Getting started
with on-line learning

Gunter Saunders

 Learning Partners

Published by Learning Partners
Suite 4 Marquis House
2 North Street
Winchcombe
Gloucestershire GL54 5LH

Telephone / Fax 01242 604060
email *lp.books@argonet.co.uk*
www.lpbooks.co.uk

© Learning Partners 2000
ISBN 1 899692 06 1   371 · 39445 (566)

Printed by AM-PM,
Windsor St, Cheltenham
Glos. GL52 2DE

To Manjula and the boys.

I would like to acknowledge the support of all of the students who have helped me to explore new approaches to course delivery.

Gunter Saunders

Publisher's Acknowledgements

The publishers gratefully acknowledge the help of all the organisations and companies who kindly gave copyright approval to show screen shots of their products or websites.

NISS is a division of EduServ who are a registered educational charity.

Netscape Communications Corporation has not authorised, sponsored, endorsed or approved this publication and is not responsible for its content. Netscape and the Netscape Communications Corporate Logos, are trademarks and trade names of Netscape Communications Corporation. All other product names and/or logos are trademarks of their respective owners.

The following trademarks are the property of the Microsoft Corporation: Microsoft® Office, Microsoft® Word, Microsoft® Excel, Microsoft® Powerpoint, Microsoft® Internet Explorer, Microsoft® Outlook, Microsoft® Frontpage, Microsoft® Windows and NT. Screenshots of Microsoft® Powerpoint reprinted by permission of Microsoft Corporation.

Contents

Chapter Five

Chapter Six

Chapter Seven

Chapter Eight

Chapter Nine

Preface

The development of Information and Communication Technology (ICT), particularly the evolution of the Internet, has provided and continues to provide many new opportunities for academic staff. A flexible set of tools with the potential to invigorate teaching and learning is available to all. After years of depression caused by increases in student numbers and the decline in the unit of resource, the interest in using ICT can be refreshing. It is important, however, right from the outset, to make clear that this book is not about convincing anyone that using ICT is a certain way to ensure a first class learning experience. Clearly, there are many excellent courses that make little use of computers or computer based material. Equally, there are extremely stimulating learning experiences available on courses that, for one reason or another, rely almost exclusively on the use of computers.

In traditional institutions of further and higher education, academic staff can usually be divided into two main groups in relation to the use of ICT. One group of staff already uses computers extensively, at a high level, to support and deliver courses. Such staff normally work either in a computer science department or closely with computer scientists, often with financial support from government schemes established to stimulate the development of on-line learning systems. The other group of staff, the majority, either does not use ICT at all or at best uses e-mail and the occasional Internet resource to improve communication and extend the material available to students.

The first group of staff referred to above wonders what all the current fuss is about, as they may have been using video-conferencing or the web or CD-ROM based material to support what they do for some time. The second group is often so in awe of the technology, and can be so blinded by the techno-talk of the former group, that they automatically assume that the business of getting started with on-line learning is beyond them. Part of the problem for this group stems from the generally poor levels of staff development in the use of

ICT. In addition, however, a lot of problems stem from the misconception that on-line learning means the provision to students of entirely free-standing computer-based material. Free-standing is used here to mean material that, in principle, enables a student to learn all or much of what is required from the computer, thus making unnecessary any extensive interaction with a tutor. Somewhere between the two extremes, of 'contact- free' delivery and basic use of e-mail and the Internet, is a third scenario. In this scenario, ICT is used extensively to support traditional courses and create more opportunities for independent, student-centred active learning.

This book is written primarily for those who would like to position themselves somewhere between the two extremes referred to above. It is intended for those in traditional institutions who wish to exploit ICT to help with the mass education system. It also aims to help staff in such institutions who, for whatever reason, are having to consider the provision of more learning support to remote locations such as the student workplace.

Given the intended audience, much of the book is targeted at the relative beginner, with the intention of showing how best to make rapid advances in using material in electronic form, both to support a course and to extend opportunities for independent and active learning. The book focuses on approaches that almost any academic should be able to make some progress with, assuming that they are working in an institution with a network connection to the Joint Academic Network (JANET) and have access to a reasonable PC. Although most of the book has been written with the beginner in mind, those who have already begun to exploit ICT for information provision will also find parts of the book useful in guiding developments that allow increased interaction with students.

It will be evident, from the beginning of Chapter 2, that there is consideration of the use of ICT to support administrative activities as well as teaching and learning, particularly at the level of individual taught modules. Whilst at first sight, given the title of the book, this might appear strange, administrative issues should be seen as an integral part of the teaching and learning function. Certainly it is true that more staff have less time to spend tutoring and preparing learning material because of the added burden of such administrative functions.

Summary The book divides into four major themes. The first is developed in Chapters 1 and 2 which examine commonly used teaching and learning approaches and take an initial look at how computers can make an impact on education. The book begins with a brief overview of current issues in teaching and learning in further and higher education (Chapter 1), before introducing some of the potential uses of ICT within this context (Chapter 2).

The second theme, in Chapters 3 and 4, is to give an easily understood overview of the hardware and software that are most commonly encountered in on-line learning. This provides a basic guide to the ICT tools the average teacher will need to know about.

The third theme focuses on the growing value and use of web technology and gives examples of the use of the World Wide Web (www), Internet and intranets (Chapters 5 and 6).

The latter four chapters have been written to enable beginners to follow the material easily, whilst moderate users of computers will find ways to carry out certain tasks more effectively.

The final theme, developed in Chapters 7 to 9, is to examine issues of managing on-line learning and the use of ICT in teaching and learning. Detailed examples of approaches to course delivery using ICT, achievable within any typical institution, are described in Chapter 7. Chapter 8 examines individual issues, such as on-line assessment, student support and guidance and the design of on-line materials.

Throughout these chapters, the emphasis is on realistically achievable but useful outcomes, although suggestions on progression are constantly made.

A detailed case study of one institution's approach to the opening up of opportunities for networked learning to all staff makes up Chapter 9. This chapter is not written primarily for academic staff but for those who lead or manage institutions. It is critical to the success of on-line learning that senior staff understand the significant role that they have to play. They can ensure the use of ICT by everyone across a university or college. It is hoped that academic staff will also find this chapter useful, serving as it does to illustrate the potential value of bringing together both management and teaching staff with shared views on how the use of ICT in teaching can and should develop.

Chapter 10 considers how ICT may be used in the future to encourage independent learning.

Approaches to learning and teaching

One

This chapter outlines the major challenges currently facing staff in further and higher education institutions. Teaching and learning approaches are briefly and broadly examined. Basic analogies between good practice in more traditional teaching methods and on-line learning approaches are drawn. The need for staff to become facilitators of the learning process is considered.

The changing face of further and higher education

It is hard to remember a time in the last 20 years, when post-compulsory education wasn't undergoing some sort of fundamental change or experiencing a new initiative that has subsequently led to change. Well over a decade ago the Tory government started the headlong expansion that resulted in a tripling or more of the number of students entering higher education. This expansion, the decline in the unit of resource, increased diversity in the student population and other related pressures such as modularisation (see Table 1 overleaf) have led staff within the sectors into difficult times. The factors shown in Table 1 have made it harder to continue with traditional methods of course delivery, creating what sometimes feels like a continuous stream of things to do.

The teaching of large classes inevitably requires fundamental changes in approach and has led to the publication of a myriad of suggestions as to how to cope. Overall, larger class sizes have meant an increased reliance on the lecture as a means of delivery. This has inevitably encouraged teacher-centred courses and reduced the active involvement of students in their own learning during classes. In addition to the impact on teaching delivery, the increase in student numbers has also had a marked effect, as one would expect, on work outside the classroom. There is, for example, more marking to do and therefore less time to provide feedback on course work to students. The effects of the increase in student numbers on the teaching function has been further compounded by the fact that students must now be provided with more basic housekeeping

Gibbs and Jenkins (1992)

Table 1   Pressures for change in further and higher education

- Increase in student numbers
- Increased diversity of the student population
- Increases in number of part-time students
- Decrease in the unit of resource
- Increased costs of learning resources
- Staffing problems related to low morale
- Increases in the number of part-time teaching staff
- Increased collaboration with other institutions
- Rapid changes in information and communications technology
- Demands from industry for increased focus on transferable (key) skills and vocational learning
- Modularisation
- Quality assurance demands
- Research assessment exercise
- Increased competition
- Increased accountability
- Semesterisation
- Development of assessment methods testing skill and competences

information for each module (e.g. module handbooks, learning outcomes) than in the past.

The major response to these pressures has been exhortations to move towards more open and independent forms of learning. The growth in use of the term Resource Based Learning (RBL) has partially stemmed from the need to respond to these. RBL serves the open, independent learning model, providing students with self-directed learning materials in many *Brown and Smith* forms. In this model of learning the student is more *(1996)* responsible for their own learning. In addition, the amount of collaborative work that they undertake with their peers is greater than that encountered in a more traditional model. RBL has required large holdings of materials, books, worksheets and primary resources. Now it is possible to package learning material in different forms (e.g. text, images, videos, audio) into one universally accessible electronic medium, the World Wide Web (www).

The model of independent, open learning is one that could create more opportunities for effective learning than is currently achievable in the crowded further and higher education systems today. To move effectively to the new model two major changes are necessary. One is that students understand that independent learning can benefit them. The other is that the lecturer's role must shift more towards that of a manager or facilitator of the learning process. A trap to avoid is that of acknowledging and allowing the change in student role without altering the expected role of the lecturer. The current reality is that many staff have inadvertently fallen into this trap.

In the new model the tutor must spend more time managing and guiding the learning process and less time talking whilst students take notes. For an open, independent learning approach to succeed, academic staff need to stop appearing as the 'sage on the stage' and instead engineer an almost constant presence as the 'guide on the side'.

Features of learning

In the past, behavioural and cognitive theories have dominated learning research. Nowadays, there are many other theories of learning that emphasise additional factors in the learning process, such as motivation and personality. Neither of these two important characteristics was significant in the formulation of either of the two early major theories. Theories of learning are really not that easy to get to grips with, and don't necessarily help change approaches to teaching and learning. It is more likely that the majority of teachers would prefer to consider practical points that can be concluded from research into teaching and learning. *Gibbs (1995)* The view of Gibbs (1995) was that fundamental research into the learning process is undertaken to 'empower teachers' and should be conducted by professional researchers. Most teachers in further and higher education are more interested in applying effective approaches that help the majority of students to learn. It is therefore important for the results of research to be communicated in a way that facilitates their application.

Some believe that a great body of research exists into the processes of teaching and learning and that the results are available for teachers to profit from. It is certainly true that much has been done to examine the teaching and learning process. But how useful has all of this work been, in a practical sense, for the majority of academic staff? For example, does this body of research allow us to define learning adequately so as to achieve a common base from which to develop teaching and learning approaches? It doesn't because learning can naturally be defined in several ways. There are a number of reasons for this including:

- students perceive learning in a number of ways
- academic staff perceive learning in a number of ways
- the government and funding councils are increasing their influence over the way that learning is perceived
- students have different learning styles
- people learn for many reasons.

Many more reasons could be listed, but those above are enough to convince most people that a widely acceptable definition of learning, and therefore in a sense teaching, is not easy to realise.

A course leader might say that successful learning means achieving the learning outcomes stated for the course or module that students are studying. To some this might seem an unacceptable definition of learning. Dedicated teachers who care about the future of their students would certainly want to know how best to enable their students to achieve the learning outcomes, provided that whichever approach was taken allowed some high level engagement with the subject matter. The average teacher, trying to do their job in the current climate, can gain support from the practical and well founded links between teaching approaches and student engagement with the subject matter.

A significant point is that students have different *Honey and Mumford* learning styles. This is important in its own right but *(1986)* also because the majority of staff understand that their students learn in different ways. Similarly, it is possible to reach broad agreement that learning by rote is not really going to enable a student to achieve the broad aims of further and higher education. Nor, indeed, will the student seeking work at the end of a course be best served by such an approach. Other statements about teaching and learning that might be considered by most to reflect their experience are shown in Table 2.

Table 2 Face value statements about teaching and learning

- Students have a variety of learning approaches/styles
- A deep learning approach is favoured by opportunities for discussion
- Students learn more when they are active
- The larger a class, the more communication becomes a one-way process
- Students respond to motivated/interested lecturers
- Students are assessment driven
- Students like face-to-face contact
- Face-to-face communication is better than electronic communication
- Students respond to a variety of teaching methods

Surface versus deep learning

Producing graduates who can solve problems, critically evaluate and communicate clearly requires much more than rote learning. Rote learning leads only to superficial understanding in most cases. Recall is typically short and ability to use the acquired knowledge in an unfamiliar environment (i.e. outside an exam room) is not well developed. Such a surface approach can of course be tempting for students to slip into, as it is related to the high workload that they experience. The degree of surface learning undertaken will also be influenced by the way that learning outcomes and assessment methods work against rote approaches.

Marton and Saljo (1984)
Biggs and Moore (1993)

The converse of surface learning is the aim of all academic staff. A number of investigations have shown that students adopting a deep rather than surface approach to their learning achieve appropriate learning outcomes more successfully, and can obtain higher marks. Deep learning normally occurs when students interact and have opportunities to think about the material. When deep learning occurs, a student will be able to place the new knowledge or information being considered within the context of the entire subject area. This can often be achieved by exercises or discussions designed to allow students to work out how a particular conclusion was reached.

Watkins and Hattie (1985)
Trigwell and Prosser (1991)

To encourage a deep approach, a number of factors must be taken into account. Reference has been made to assessment. Students are not surprisingly assessment driven and examinations that require only regurgitation of notes will obviously support a surface approach to learning. For effective deep learning to occur, in addition to the right kind of learning outcomes and assessment, it is vital that students are motivated and excited by the teacher and teaching approach. If staff give the impression of being information providers only, then students will adapt to that, mostly by taking a surface approach. Motivation, although not impossible to gain from lectures, is more often evident in discussion and activity sessions.

When the terms 'surface' and 'deep' learning were introduced some years ago, some staff greeted them with a degree of contempt, considering them to represent new fangled approaches to course delivery. Curiously, however, when the same staff describe their approach to teaching, they invariably paint a picture that is synonymous with the approaches designed to facilitate deep learning. The conclusion is that most teachers would probably agree that students learn more when they are actively involved in discussing, analysing and challenging the subject matter. Like many of us, they prefer, however, to reach a conclusion themselves, using their own terminology, rather than have something apparently strange thrust upon them.

Some typical teaching approaches There is considerable disagreement amongst both researchers and lecturers over what is or is not effective as a learning/teaching approach. What is generally agreed, however, is that it is best to use a variety of teaching methods with any group of students. A reason to use variety is the fact that, as mentioned earlier, different students will have different learning styles. Whilst some will prefer to sit and listen during lectures, others will need to scribble notes continuously. In small group discussions some students will dominate, not always because they are naturally pushy, but sometimes because they need to be very active in order to learn. Similarly, students who are very quiet during discussion sessions could be shy or they could simply be the type who prefer to hear the views of others before voicing their own. Some typical learning styles encountered during small group/problem solving sessions are shown in Table 3. In all practical situations it is impossible to find time to tailor a course for each individual according

Table 3   Some typical learning styles found amongst students
(Honey and Mumford 1986)

Student learning style	Characteristics
Activist	'I'll try anything at least once' approach to problem solving. Likes to get there quickly with the minimum of fuss.
Reflector	Sifts through all data carefully, listens to all views before stating their own.
Theorist	Typically ill at ease with subjective analyses and lateral thinking. Keen on principles and basic assumptions.
Pragmatist	Likes to put recently learned theories into practice. Has a very practical, down-to-earth approach.

to their own learning style. Hence the shotgun approach of using a variety of teaching styles and exercises so that most students on a course will find some sessions particularly enjoyable and useful. Some teaching approaches that should be familiar to most and the kinds of learning outcome that they might each facilitate are shown in Table 4.

Table 4   Teaching methods and associated learning outcomes

Teaching approach	Potential learning outcomes
Lectures, textbooks, handouts, information retrieval	Mainly for the development of knowledge and some understanding.
Guided private study, open learning materials	Can be especially useful for personal development, the management of learning and the development of independence.
Case studies, laboratory classes, work experience, essay writing	Development of the ability to use information together with ideas to reach solutions and/or solve problems.
Research projects	As above plus development of critical analytical skills. Provide opportunities to compare opposing views and put forward theories.
Discussion/debating sessions, seminars and oral presentations	Development of the capability to argue a case with peers, to generate ideas and develop communication skills.
Peer/self assessment, learning logs	Personal development and experience of the management of learning.
Group exercises	Development of team working skills.

Lecturing The lecture is still current as a major vehicle for teaching. Interestingly, most of those who advocate the value of the lecture would also support the idea that students learn best and most during discussions rather than lectures. All this suggests that lecturers should be trying to reduce the amount of lecturing they do, possibly looking for alternative ways to provide interactive exercises during classroom sessions. In recent years, the amount of lecturing has probably increased.

There is plenty of evidence, from a number of research investigations, to show that lecturing compares unfavourably with other approaches in terms of enabling students to achieve the full range of learning outcomes *Bligh (1971)* that education is required to effect. As a means of educational delivery it is expedient, well known and an understandably easy way to deal with a large class. It is also a trap, however, because the nature of communication is such that the lecture can mean that the audience does no thinking about the topic at all. Equally, for the lecturer, it can mean that they do not think as much as they would like and neither do they learn as much as they could. To the dedicated teaching practitioner this may ultimately mean that they come to dislike what they do. Lecturers often wonder whether their students do any thinking at all. It may be worth turning that question around and considering how much thinking a lecturer does during a lecture.

Even those who argue strongly against the lecture as a means to bring about optimal learning do not view every lecture as a bad educational experience. There are a variety of lecturing styles that can be very effective, going some way towards meeting the objective of realising deep learning. Most teaching staff consider lectures to be extremely useful in circumstances where there is a need to place a topic in the context of an overall course or when there has been a significant advance in subject knowledge that has only just been published. For example, many universities mounted extra lectures for students at the time Watson and Crick published their landmark work in order to ensure that new graduates were as up to date as possible. Equally, the worldwide moratorium on genetic engineering in the early 1970s was readily communicated to students via lectures as up-to-the-minute relevant knowledge to those about to graduate.

The modern electronic age allows the dissemination of advances in knowledge much more widely and quickly than was possible when Watson and Crick were publishing their findings. Accessibility to the latest information is important. As a consequence, there should be more opportunity, during the highly valued face-to-face contact that both students and staff can enjoy and benefit from, to discuss the implications of latest findings rather than just hear about them.

Making a lecture work well In his book Bligh (1971) supports the view that lectures are good for imparting information but that little evidence exists to show that lectures can help students learn to think. Indeed, Bligh advocates a mixed approach to teaching where periods of *'chalk and talk'* are broken up by exercises involving individual or, more typically, groups of students. These exercises are intended to reinforce and/or clarify any learning that has occurred whilst the lecturer was speaking. Some lecturing approaches, specifically developed to help deal with larger classes, use a mixed approach along the lines advocated by Bligh. These days it is to be hoped that students only occasionally experience long unbroken lectures, with no opportunity for input from them. There is some evidence to suggest, however, that the compulsive lecturer does still exist and that, on the whole, students do not value even a 50 minute non-stop lecture.

Proponents of the lecture method often quickly point out that lecturing provides the opportunity for sharing enthusiasm for the subject matter. Many studies have shown that students have positive things to say about lectures, provided that they perceive them to be

Bliss and Ogborn interesting and stimulating. It is clear that, for a lecture *(1977)* to have a sustained effect on learning, the enthusiasm of *Beard and Senior* the lecturer is important but is not all that is required. *(1980)* Students need basic help to learn and some need more help than others. For example, it is useful for students to know what the key points of a lecture are. If the lecturer emphasises these key points, then students should be able to follow the lecture more readily. A handout accompanying the lecture, that has the key points on it, can also provide a useful framework for note taking.

All too often a lecturer can fail to explain clearly whether the lecture is intended primarily to provide facts that must be recalled precisely (common in science) or to provide a broad overview of a topic. The intended purpose can influence the type of note taking required. One of the major potential failings of lectures is related to what students do within the first 24 hours of having written their notes. It is vital that some follow-up activity is used to reinforce the material covered in the lecture. If there is no timetabled activity shortly after the lecture, then it is essential to persuade students of the importance of reviewing and editing their notes as soon as they can. If they do not, the value of the lecture in terms of learning outcomes will rapidly diminish.

Hartley (1983)
McCleish (1976)

The point is that any learning event, be it a lecture, group work (see below) or some on-line activity, requires provision of support and guidance in order to ensure that a majority of students will learn effectively.

Tutorials, seminars and group discussion

In addition to the lecture, teachers in further and higher education have always traditionally used the tutorial or seminar as a way to promote the effectiveness of lectures. Since quite often the terms tutorial and seminar are used interchangeably, it is probably simplest to aggregate non-lecture classroom sessions under the general heading of discussion or, perhaps more accurately, group discussion. In a typical course running 20 years ago, a lecture (perhaps lasting one to one and a half hours) would be followed by a tutorial session designed to reinforce or support the information delivered in the lecture. With a large class there would probably have been several tutorial groups each of a size that was manageable for one member of staff. Today, this is often no longer possible for a variety of reasons, including some mismatch between staff expertise and popular subjects that have emerged in recent years. Instead, it is proving increasingly necessary to rely on students to work independently or in groups, helping one another. There is no doubt, especially in diverse classes that are currently the norm, that students can be very effective at helping one another understand difficult concepts. Although this type of approach is to be welcomed in some respects, there is the risk that a group of students can go off up a 'blind alley', led perhaps by the enthusiasm (rather than the intellectual ability) of one group member. Thus, as in all group work, effective staff involvement, or at least the provision of some training and guidance to students about approaches to group work, is essential. Student group work is

Goodlad (1989)
Jaques (1991)

increasingly being used as a way to break up long time-tabled sessions and as a means to provide some training in transferable skills. Despite changes in the approach to bringing about opportunities for discussion of a topic, there is no doubt that, for the committed student, discussion sessions remain an invaluable route to achieving better understanding of a topic.

In science, group discussions often revolve around solving problems. These are typically set to check that students can apply the knowledge that they were meant to absorb in a lecture or group of lectures. However, a problem with such sessions is that they can appear to the students to be too much like a test that is imposed on them. The value of such sessions to the student who didn't understand the topic in the first place may well be minimal. Potentially more valuable is an approach that gives students the opportunity to brainstorm a topic so as to allow them to establish which aspects or parts of a *Boud and Felleti* topic they don't fully comprehend before they are *(1991)* presented with problem-solving sessions.

Self study Self study has always been a critical element of education and its significance is likely to grow from now on. It is perhaps not surprising to find a plethora of self study misconceptions amongst students. Reading provides a good example. So many students need help to understand that when studying a topic, one need not necessarily read every word on that topic in the course textbook. The purpose of any particular reading needs to be put in context by the reader in order for the reading to serve its learning purpose. Students understandably benefit from some guidance on such matters as reading approaches, but seldom get any. There is no doubt that an increase in the use of on-line learning material will require some considerable re-education on the part of both staff and students in terms of appropriate study skills. The cycle of lecture: note taking: revision: exam will obviously no longer work as a model and should not be replaced simply by lecture note handouts: revision: exam.

On-line learning As stated earlier, it is hard to reach consensus on a definition of learning. Equally, attempting to define on-line learning can be difficult. This is partly because on-line learning can come in many guises and has many terms. Thus, computer- based learning, computer-assisted learning, multimedia, computer-aided learning or web-based learning, for example, can all be used at various times to sum up one particular flavour of on-line learning. This plethora of terminology, allied to the pace of change in ICT systems, can lead anyone to have a vision of on-line learning that is characterised by a computer entirely replacing the role of a lecturer.

Often, in this limited vision, on-line learning is seen as something that enables a period of fully interactive dialogue between student and computer. This conjures up an image of an on-line learning event where a student sits in front of a computer screen, making informed choices and being automatically provided with comment and feedback on their choices by the computer. Some of the feedback or comment could be expected to be in the form of process simulations, the modelling of systems or instant assessment. Such a vision imposes a far too narrow definition of on-line learning to enable, in the short or medium term, the bulk of staff in further and higher education to get deeply involved.

A more pragmatic approach is to consider that on-line learning encompasses all use of computers and associated software to enable the delivery of material in such a way as to enhance the overall effectiveness of learning. In such a model of on-line learning, the simple use of e-mail to maintain regular contact with a student can be a way of using computers to enhance the learning process. At a time when the whole world is being excited by information technology and what it can do, it is a mistake to take a minority off into a virtual world of learning, when the majority could benefit from the proper implementation of fundamental computing possibilities.

Traditional versus on-line learning

Since this book is primarily about on-line learning, it is sensible to ask whether it is worth considering what has been established from traditional approaches to course delivery. The answer is yes, it is worth considering, because on-line learning is also about providing information and subsequent scope for analysis and practical use of that and other information. The difference can simply be that the unidirectional information delivery part of the process occurs via electronic means and that face-to-face events serve an entirely different purpose.

In on-line learning, valuable face-to-face time should be spent as far as possible on discussion that actively reinforces both the on-line information provided and any supporting on-line exercises.

One important misconception to dispel is that good on-line learning material is significantly different from any other form of good learning material. Table 5 lists a range of features that are considered to be important in the design of on-line learning materials. All are equally applicable to the material or approaches that the majority of staff in further and higher education utilise now.

The way in which on-screen material looks is excluded from Table 5. This is an area where on-line learning needs some attention. These aspects, the use of particular fonts, colours, etc., will be dealt with in Chapter 7

As the subsequent chapters of this book will show, there need be little difference between what is good practice in on-line learning and learning through traditional courses. Just as students need guidance to make the most of traditional teaching approaches, so too will they need help with on-line material. All that is needed to realise the potential benefits of electronic technology is a sufficient grasp of the basic technology itself. With this, any reflective teaching practitioner should be able to use technology to aid the learning process.

Table 5   Important features in on-line learning material

- Are there clearly stated aims and objectives?
- Is the relationship(s) between different parts of the course clearly brought out?
- Is the learner able to find out easily where they are in the course?
- Are there easy to follow signposts to additional material?
- Are learners able to progress logically through the material?
- Are there quality assurance procedures in place?
- Does the material seek to motivate the learner?
- Are there relevant examples or case studies for learners to work through?
- Can the learner interact with the material or the producers of the material?
- Is there any self assessment built in?
- Is there any feedback built in or provided?
- Are there learning outcomes?
- Is there guidance for the learner about how to approach using the material?
- Are there opportunities for face-to-face support?
- Are there opportunities for learners to collaborate in exercises?
- Is the language used appropriate to the learner?

Summary

- Several factors are currently combining to force higher and further education to examine approaches to teaching and learning.
- Lectures can be good in certain circumstances and if delivered in the right way.
- Most students learn more when they are actively engaged with the subject matter, e.g. through group work.
- Computers can change teaching and learning approaches.
- Students need to be convinced that learning by rote will not serve them best in the long term.
- Students need guidance to make the most of any type of learning event.
- Academic staff should consider abandoning the role of 'sage on the stage' in favour of becoming a 'guide on the side'.

The role of computers and computer networks in further and higher education

TWO

This chapter examines the underlying reasons for the current intense interest in the use of computers and information technology in education. It also considers the various levels to which computer use can be taken. The major forms of information dissemination via electronic means are discussed in terms of their relative potential contribution to teaching, learning, administrative functions and general communication.

The information technology revolution

Brooks (1997)

There is currently considerable hype surrounding the use of ICT in further and higher education. High profile developments, such as the creation of the University for Industry and the recent government announcement of plans for an e-university to serve the international market, are building an appreciable 'ICT in Education' momentum. Cynical staff, perhaps finding it difficult to even consider change, may choose to believe that institutions will support the high profile currently surrounding ICT only as long as there are various ICT related pots of money to bid for. This was certainly the case with the Enterprise Initiative that provided significant funding for institutions to get work-related exercises for students off the ground. Once special funding ceases, a stated institutional desire to change can evaporate. There are several major differences about the current focus on ICT in education that distinguish it from other significant changes or initiatives that the sector has experienced.

Most lecturers have worked out for themselves that there are a number of good reasons to consider using computers. Those most commonly cited on training about using the Internet in teaching are:

- a belief that its use could be of benefit to both students and staff
- the desire to reach a new market or more of the same market
- the desire to fundamentally change teaching and learning approaches
- future students will come to expect it.

At an institutional level, both bespoke providers of distance learning courses and traditional institutions have good reason to take the ICT revolution seriously. The former have their markets to protect. Most providers of distance courses are doubtless already on top of the possibilities for reduction in costs afforded, for example, by the use of web-based technologies. More traditional organisations have the opportunity to use ICT, not only to increase their share of the distance learning market, but also to support existing delivery to students who will continue to attend a place of study. Indeed, traditional institutions currently have a big advantage on their side, in terms of the development of distance courses. No one would disagree with the importance of face-to-face contact to distance learners. Traditional institutions have experienced staff who can provide such support, whereas distance learning organisations may have to tout for such staff as and when they need to. A major advantage that distance providers have is their experience of structuring a course or learning package appropriately to the distance dimension.

It is also important to remember that the same electronic tools that lecturers can now use for educational delivery are an increasingly familiar part of the lives of most of further and higher education's customers. They are, after all, used for many modern day activities. This means that students are increasingly going to feel part of any ICT-related revolution that the teaching profession goes through. Sooner or later the majority of students will expect to experience electronic communication routinely in institutions and will be surprised if computers are not used wherever it is sensible and feasible to use them. The whole world is experiencing the electronic age: it is not a change peculiar to pedagogists.

The ICT revolution is likely to have as big an effect on central administrative tasks in colleges and universities. Computers provide a number of new approaches to dealing with some of the massively demoralising and time-consuming problems commonly encountered by administrative and academic staff. The scale of the potential impact can be realised simply by considering the range of information with which students need to be provided. Some of the information that students typically require from both academic staff and central departments is shown in Table 6. Computers are increasingly being used across the sector to provide such information to students and potential students.

Table 6   Areas where ICT provision enhances available support

- Lecture notes
- Timetables
- Syllabuses
- Past examination papers
- Learning outcomes
- Model examination answers
- Course work details
- Course work submission
- Communicating with tutors
- Discussion groups
- Course regulations
- Health and safety
- Careers and part-time employment
- Automatic module enrolment
- Registration for examinations
- Student support information

It is clear from Table 6 that there are many good reasons for considering the use of ICT to support the delivery of courses. There is another commonly encountered reason that acts as a powerful driving force behind the desire for individuals to use ICT, and that is the technology. This reason, which is basically to use technology simply because it is there, should be avoided. Any large-scale development in the use of computers should go ahead only if it is going to help to make course delivery more effective and enjoyable, in a pedagogical or student-centred sense. Whilst certain types of technology, such as video-conferencing, have obvious instant excitement and appeal, there are many other approaches involving ICT that will currently reap greater benefits because they are more widely applicable.

The level of computer use

Computers have been playing a significant role in education for a number of years, starting in the 60s and 70s with the emerging use of mainframes across a wide number of subject areas. Until the advent of the personal computer, however, they were largely the domain of central computing services and computer science departments. As PCs have become more accessible, their use to support teaching and administrative functions within institutions has grown.

As a means of providing information, computers and computer networks can be fast and reliable. It is possible to use computers to do more than simply provide information. Users can interact with computers to varying degrees and for a variety of purposes in the development of on-line learning material.

Interaction is a good way to illustrate the significance of the time factor. The amount of time, effort and, to some extent, skill required to produce on-line material is directly proportional to the degree of computer-based interaction that the material will have built into it. Interactive computer-based exercises are intended to be completed by a student working on their own in front of a monitor (or collaboratively with peers in front of several monitors). Ideally, the student receives feedback instantly on the answers they provide during such an exercise. Equally, the path that the student follows through the exercise may be influenced by the answers that they give. Such exercises take a great deal of time and planning to develop. It is, however, important to understand that on-line support for a traditional course need not necessarily entail the development, at least initially, of any interactive computer-based exercises of the type described above.

Saunders et al. (1999)

The need to provide a stand-alone computer for individual interaction can be of greater urgency for the provision of modern distance learning courses. Even in this model of learning, however, it is not essential to develop multimedia-based interactive material immediately in order for computers to make an impact. Certainly, as mentioned in Chapter 1, computers can benefit resource-based learning approaches by providing a single route through which to make a range of media types available.

Although computers afford a multitude of possibilities, it is important in any practical approach to distinguish between what is possible and what is feasible for the majority. This chapter and those that follow will do this because the most critical factor in the success or failure of ICT in the future of course delivery will be time. The time needed by staff to make available valuable learning material in electronic form will determine the level to which individuals will take their use of ICT. In the next few years, many will find ways to use computers to support the delivery of a traditional course, probably without changing the nature of course delivery very much. A few will head instantly into the realms of interactive multimedia, possibly seeking to change the nature of a course almost overnight. As later chapters will demonstrate, it is possible, even without stand-alone multimedia material, to change the delivery of a course radically.

In summary, whether you are in a traditional institution, you provide distance courses or have been exploiting resource-based learning methodology, if you believe in the value of independent learning as a model for the future, then computers can help. With a positive attitude, the time needed to get started will not add significantly to the burden typically faced each year of the updating of handouts and other learning materials.

Using computers to help staff and support students

There are many features of teaching, whether primarily in a traditional, resource-based or purely distance learning environment, that can be undertaken more efficiently via the use of computer networks. Equally, administrative functions stand to benefit considerably by investing in more computer-based transactions.

Providers of distance learning courses are now in the position of being able to produce and distribute their wares on modern media with an ease not dreamed of even five years ago. Many departments are already experiencing a reduction in costs as, instead of posting a large hard copy volume to students, they send a CD-ROM or direct their students to a web site. In addition, it is relatively simple and feasible for providers of distance education to interact with their students via e-mail and World Wide Web (www) based forms.

Both e-mail and the www provide a means for students to submit course work and for lecturers to return feedback. It is becoming constantly easier to video-conference over the www and it is only a matter of time before it becomes routine for us to see and talk to others over long distances.

The www is now dominating discussions on how best to disseminate information to students, whilst at the same time eliciting interaction and feedback. Not too many years ago the CD-ROM was the medium through which computer-based delivery of courses could occur. As stated previously, the rapid development of web technology now allows much of the multimedia, characteristic of CD-ROM based material, to be directly embedded in web pages. Table 7 compares the merits of three types of electronic communication for their use in teaching.

Table 7   Advantages and disadvantages of three types of electronic communication

	Advantages	Disadvantages/Problems
e-mail	Can remain in contact over a distance; can communicate with more than just immediate classmates and staff; useful for housekeeping issues and can ensure contact with tutor.	Currently not everyone uses e-mail or trusts it; limited in terms of delivery of interactive material.
CD-ROM	Less bulky than text-based material; can be 3-D and very interactive; allows for some non-linearity in approach.	Time-consuming to produce/write the material; necessary to produce and issue new CD when updating.
www or Internet	As above but is truly non-linear; inexpensive (currently); relatively easy to make certain type of material; with networked material need to update only one copy.	Not everyone can currently gain satisfactory access; heavily interactive elements can only be used with state of the art computers.

A common question asked on ICT training courses is *'Will computers put me out of a job'*? Others have the view that the sector is at greater risk, in terms of job loss, if it fails to grasp the nettle with respect to ICT. It is more likely that computers will change the teacher's role rather than replace it. Those who are worried might consider the experience of the Americans in the use of ICT in education. They have a saying, *'high-tech means high touch'*. This reflects the finding that, generally, the more technology that is introduced into a taught programme, the more students want to have interaction

Forsyth (1998) with the tutor. There is no doubt that the majority of today's students do not want to lose their opportunities for face-to-face meetings with teaching staff. So, the

Saunders et al. (1999) likely role of computers for the foreseeable future is as an adjunct to current methods of delivery. For example, computer-based delivery can help to create more opportunities for active learning in classroom sessions.

Another common question is *'Will computers replace the lecture'*? It would certainly not be a bad idea to replace some types of lecture with a better event, which could, for example, be a combination of on-line material plus some form of discussion.

Bligh (1971) With respect to administrative functions, there does seem to be much greater scope (and some would say desire) for reducing the need for face-to-face contact and indeed for the completion of many paper forms. It is important, though, to make a distinction between administrative information provided by central departments and the administrative functions related to individual module management. Much of the latter is the remit of the academic and therefore we will confine ourselves in this and later chapters largely to discussing how ICT can help in the day-to-day running of modules.

So how can computers help in a traditional institution and how can they be used to relieve some of the pressures that have built up with the expansion in student numbers? In theory, computers can do the lot. Table 8 shows how computers can impact on the day-to- day business of lecturers. You can talk to people via computers, you can play sound and video and, of course, you can produce limitless amounts of text and still images. The text and associated images can be

Table 8   Areas of activity where computers can have an impact

Activity	Use, contribution and advantages of ICT
Classroom activities	Provision of material to support more interactive classroom-based exercises; replacement of some classroom sessions with computer-based material appropriate for independent learning; provision of wide source of additional information of relevance; laboratory and other simulations.
Preparation of visual aids	Use of electronic slide shows facilitating rapid updating of visual aids for the support of taught classes; possible to incorporate wide range of interactivity.
Preparation of printed material (hand outs)	Availability of 'handout' material in electronic form reduces the amount of paper and photocopying that staff need to do.
Personal tutoring/counselling and communicating with students/colleagues	Use of e-mail makes it easier to ensure that students can get a message through to tutors and vice versa; e-mail can reduce the need for paper communications with colleagues and can lead to/generate healthy and rapid discussion of issues.
Provision of module/course specific information (e.g. timetables etc.)	Reduces the problems associated with students who don't attend in the first week; provides interested students with information well in advance of the start of a module/course; supports students who lose or can't find relevant material when they need it; facilitates communication of changes in schedule/timetable; can reduce the amount of paper needed.
Assessment	Possible reduction of assessment load via the use of automatic marking systems, e.g. for multiple choice tests; potential to provide self tests for students with automatic feedback possible.
Research	Mainly information to support research, in the form of web sites and databases.

linked together, so that readers can move between different documents and events rapidly (see Chapter 5). This is a very significant feature of the www that contrasts with the more traditional information source, the book. With its serial presentation, a book does not allow one to readily make cross-subject moves to find relevant, related material, without having access to another book. As we will see later, however, the large subject space of the Internet can lead to problems in attempting to guide student study.

It is perhaps important to note, if only to preserve a sense of reality, that there are two things that computers cannot currently do that may be important. They don't allow you to smell or to taste the contents of your computer screen (although there is ongoing research that will eventually allow this). A number of other interactions are feasible, however.

Pescovitz (1999)

For teaching purposes, computers provide a terrific source of support for students. The provision, for example, of lecture notes can help cope with some of the problems associated with the diversity of student population. There will be times when students, for legitimate reasons, cannot attend a timetabled class. The availability of some lecture notes on an accessible computer or computer network at least means that they will be able to obtain some basic information on the topic they have missed. This also provides some relief for the lecturer, who does not have to find other means to provide students who have not attended with the necessary information.

As indicated earlier in this chapter, the provision of information is a general area where the use of electronic media can pay off significantly. For every module taught, there will be a number of pieces of information that a lecturer will need to provide to all students. These include, for example, the timetable, details of course work, learning outcomes, perhaps the syllabus, and maybe even some of the course work itself. To give out hard copies of all of these items only works really well if all students attend the first week of a module (often not the case in the diverse schemes of today). Equally, even if you manage to give out all the requisite handouts to the majority of students, some will lose the most relevant pieces or will not have them to hand when they most need them. A network containing such information can be of tremendous benefit to students and staff. Not only will you find that students are not knocking on your office door to request information they should have received weeks earlier, but you also only have one copy of your timetable to update at any one time. This latter point is one of the major advantages of on-line publishing and will be discussed further in Chapter 6. Some will doubtless be worried that reference to 'reduced knocking on doors by students' implies a desire to adopt a hands-off approach. In the constrained system of today, however, the less time wasted on providing purely housekeeping information should mean that there will be more time available for academic issues.

One of the criticisms often raised of the posting of lecture notes is that some students will consider that possession of the lecture notes will enable them to pass the module. This assumes that a rote learning approach is prevalent. If the on-line lecture notes are used as a way to facilitate active learning in timetabled sessions, the committed student will reap significant benefits. We shall return to this issue of non-interactive on-line teaching information and its value in Chapter 7.

It is difficult to consider all possible applications for ICT within any institution and the preceding parts of this chapter outline the most obvious and common. Each institution or department would be able to find functions that could benefit by being computerised. Finding the most significant problems that need solving within an institution or department will only begin to happen when a culture of change towards ICT has been initiated and stimulated. An example will help to illustrate this. At the University of Westminster it is hard for a module or course leader to maintain effective contact with the right students. This is difficult because of the diverse nature of the student population and also because of the multi-site nature of the institution. A recent institution-wide project, drawing on advances in the general awareness and use of ICT by all staff, has started to develop a simple on-line messaging system.

By using the relationship between web pages and databases, it will soon be possible for a member of staff to send a message to a predefined group of students via a web browser. The next time any students on the circulation list (which could be established by module or course or tutorial group) log on to a computer within the university, the message sent by the member of staff will automatically appear to them in a web browser window. Such potentially effective means of communicating with students will be a tremendous boost to both pedagogic and personal support. Its need was obvious, but the possibilities for achieving it were not, until the use of ICT began to be widely discussed.

Learner support and guidance With any form of learning it is sensible to provide students with some support and guidance in relation to the material covered. In traditional settings, most lecturers do not simply start lecturing, stop and then go away. Frequently, a lecturer will provide handouts that are intended to alert a student to the most important points of a teaching session. Similarly, during a lecture, clear statements such as *'this part is particularly significant'* can be made or a simple change in tone of voice or emphasis can serve to highlight critical parts. On-line learning is no different from the traditional example cited above. It is just as important with material on a CD-ROM or on the Internet to make sure that students have some help in determining the key elements of a topic and that they are provided with some information that makes it easier to appreciate where they are positioned within the broader picture of their subject area. This type of guidance is fairly easy to mimic on-line. For example, text in lecture notes, can be emphasised, where necessary, in a variety of ways or reference to or access to further information can help to guide learners through especially difficult parts. In addition, it is often easy to ensure that the body of a lecture or packet of information is placed into context and that learners are provided with guidance on what they might do next. As a minimum, any form of on-line material should:

- enable a student to gauge what they already know or should already know

- provide recommended next steps in the learning programme
- permit some element of self assessment and monitoring
- provide opportunities to go beyond the confines of any one learning package

The *'knowing your way around'* guidance described above is important but cannot, of course, ensure that the learner will understand, although it should be said that the availability of the Internet does now mean that it is relatively straightforward to provide many routes to further help. That notwithstanding, at times dependent upon the individual learner, interactive support will be necessary to achieve a complete understanding of a topic or indeed how a topic fits into the broader picture.

In a traditional learning environment, detailed pedagogic guidance is provided through the tutorial or seminar route. In many cases, however, timetabled tutorials and seminars are set up on the basis of predicting aspects that students might find difficult to grasp. This kind of learning event is not necessarily flexible enough to cater for the individual need. An alternative, the one-to-one tutorial, still occurs in some institutions, although its use for strictly academic discussions may have been superseded to a degree by an increasing need to find time for students' personal and financial problems.

On-line learning presents a series of new challenges to the provision of guidance and support. It is foolhardy to believe that providing a course via some form of electronic medium will reduce the need for forms of interaction with staff and indeed with other students. In a recent study of on-line provision, the overwhelming view of providers was that face-to-face contact with

Hurley (2000) tutors is desirable whenever possible. Where it is not possible, as in some purely distance courses, then alternative forms of interactive guidance need to be developed. Such alternatives might involve the use of e-mail or the telephone, for example. Increasingly, however, such interactive support will be provided via video-conferencing systems.

In a traditional institution, the need for alternative ways to provide academic guidance around on-line support materials will clearly not be so great. In principle, a student at a modern further or higher education institution, benefiting from the availability of on-line materials, should be able to access face-to-face support as they currently do. It is worth noting again, however, that the personal tutorial, which might still be considered by some to be the normal model for dealing with individual problems of understanding, is no longer a realistic option in many institutions. Quite commonly now, when students seek out an academic because of a problem of understanding, all that is possible is to point the student in the direction of other sources of information that might help them. It is to be hoped that a move towards increased use of independent on-line learning materials may eventually free up valuable academic staff time for the critical purpose of tutorial type activity. The scale of the current problem, however, may mean that traditional institutions can ill afford to ignore the potential of technology in facilitating a degree of interactive guidance. E-mail is being used increasingly to provide some guidance to students and this is a reasonably straightforward approach that most academic staff could start using immediately if they wished. Similarly, forms of electronic discussion can provide means for students to support each other and it is becoming possible to build up a database of frequently asked questions to be used as a first option by students requiring help. Whilst a medium-term model for the future in traditional institutions might be reduced lecturing, increased provision of information on-line and more tutorials, it should be borne in mind that the on-line environment does offer some potential to provide interactive support and guidance in its own right.

Summary

- The information technology revolution will not go away, so there is little point in *'burying one's head in the sand'*.
- There are various levels of computer-assisted learning.
- There are several simple ways to use computers and networks to support or change traditional course delivery.
- The www is making a great impact on the provision of distance courses.
- The use of computers and information technology will have as big an impact on administrative functions as on teaching and learning practice.
- Computer networks offer tremendous scope to make communication within a large, diverse student population much more effective.

Computer hardware and peripherals

Three

This chapter considers the basic components that come together to make a computer work. Computer peripherals such as printers and scanners are also examined. The ICT requirements of the average academic are defined. Practical advice on the hardware required to perform particular functions is provided.

Academic staff and ICT

http://www.ucisa.ac.uk/

http://ferl.becta.org.uk/

Most full-time staff in universities will have access to a computer in their office. Even part-time staff are likely to share a desktop computer. The latest UCISA management statistics available (1998/99) puts the ratio of computer workstations (PCs and Macintosh) to academic staff at 0.94. In further education, a slightly different picture is painted by a recent (April 1999) survey into information and communications technology in further education. The survey, carried out by the British Education Communications and Technology Agency (BECTA), puts the median PC:member of staff ratio at 1:6. The same survey reports that 37% of PCs are up to date whilst 25% are considered obsolescent.

In the majority of cases, in universities and colleges, the computer on a desk will be a PC rather than a Macintosh. The BECTA survey, referred to above, puts the percentage of computers in colleges that are PCs at around 93%. The situation in universities is probably similar, with Macintosh computers largely confined to art/design departments. It is likely, given that all universities and colleges have some form of Internet access, that most desktop computers will be networked and therefore that the majority of academic staff will use PCs to send e-mail and browse the World Wide Web. In addition, desktop PCs are likely to be loaded with most of the software types listed in Table 9 and discussed in more detail in Chapter 4.

The figures above suggest that the majority of academic staff should be able to access some sort of computer which they can use to support course delivery. Naturally, however, the ease with which any individual can begin to utilise ICT in teaching will depend on the currency of the particular computer that can be accessed. More crucial, though, is not so much the quality of the PC, but rather the capability of members of staff to fully understand the possibilities that ICT can afford them.

It is likely that most academic staff (excluding, of course, those in computer science departments) only have a general understanding of:

- what actually happens inside a computer
- the latest in terms of computer performance
- the latest in software developments.

It is not essential to have a deep understanding of the 'box of tricks' that enables a desktop computer to perform the functions that many now take for granted. It is, however, useful to have some fundamental idea of the basic components of a personal computer. This is of value if only to have some understanding on which to speak with experts charged with the responsibility of assisting in the maintenance and development of staff computers. The major components that combine to make a PC function are shown in Figure 1, together with a brief explanation of the function that the components perform.

Apart from physical components, personal computers also need software to be of use. The principal forms of software that are of use to educators are discussed in the next chapter.

Experience suggests that the average academic (in ICT terms) is wary about the whole issue of using ICT and multimedia in teaching. This may be because they believe that ICT is just another gimmick that will have its day before a return to 'traditional' methods of course delivery. Alternatively, it might be because they are a little embarrassed at knowing so little about ICT systems, probably less than their students, and would rather steer clear of it if possible. An additional problem is the misconception that, if computer-based material is not interactive in its own right, then it is not much use. In the next chapter we shall return to the use and importance of ICT.

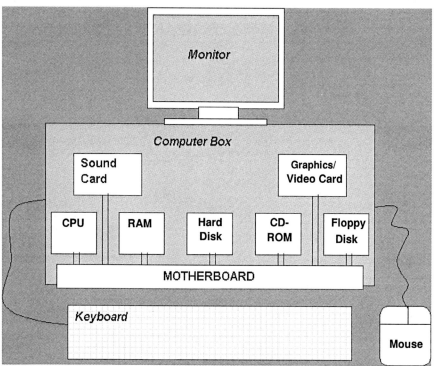

Figure 1 The components that enable a PC to work

Hard disk - This stores the operating system of the computer as well as software which is used routinely. Hard drives are made up of magnetic disks that can turn at between 3,000 and 5,000 rpm.

Motherboard - The main circuit board within a computer into which all other devices, e.g. chips or sound cards, connect.

RAM - The short-term memory of a computer. The CPU (see below) uses the RAM to hold software applications temporarily when in use. This speeds up processing. The higher the amount of RAM (measured in megabytes) in a computer, the faster it will work.

Sound card - A computer needs a sound card in order to be able to play back and record music, voice and sound effects.

Graphics or video card - The graphics card inside the computer determines the quality and sharpness of an image. This takes instructions from the CPU and produces signals that work the monitor's electron gun producing an image.

CPU - The central processing unit is the brain of a computer. CPUs run at different speeds, measured in megahertz.

Ethernet card or modem - Used to enable a computer to connect to the Internet.

Personal computers For most staff there will be little choice of computer used at work. An institution may provide its staff with a computer desktop that would probably have been chosen according to their institutional policy. It is unlikely that it will have been chosen with a view to it being used directly to prepare and deliver teaching material, unless it is very new indeed. At any one moment, it is going to be difficult for an institution to give everyone even a 15-month-old machine. Some institutions may choose to provide top class resource rooms, where staff can go to undertake advanced ICT work not possible with the PCs found in most staff offices. More institutions are moving towards the development of shared resource centres, as the cost of continually upgrading every PC becomes prohibitive. This has been prompted largely by the predicted future increase in the number of academic staff who wish to do more than standard word processing, spreadsheet work and send or receive e-mail.

What can be done if the available PCs are unsuitable for the development of teaching and learning materials? If what an individual or group is seeking to achieve with computers is closely related to the ethos and institutional outlook on information technology it may be possible to convince a school or departmental head to invest in a few new computers. It is most likely that a central or local computer support unit will be responsible for placing the order. Whoever is seeking the new computer should make sure that they speak to the support staff in order that the computer ordered is matched to its likely use, with some scope for later upgrading. This is especially important if the computer is to be used to develop teaching and learning material.

Peripherals and additional hardware Most new computers come with at least a standard floppy drive, a CD drive, sound system and a mouse. Many also now arrive with a DVD drive. Some additional peripherals or features that might also be useful at a later date are listed in Table 9.

Table 9   Hardware or peripherals and their uses

Class	Type	Features and use
Printers	Laser	Used to produce hard copies. Laser colour printers still prohibitively expensive.
	Inkjet	Inkjet printers allow affordable colour printing on a range of media, including transparencies.
Memory devices	Zip drive	Allows use of zip disks that can store 100k Mb information on magnetic tape (approximately the capacity of 70 floppy disks). Can be integral or external.
	LS120 drive	Similar to the above except storage capacity slightly higher. In addition LS120 drives will also accept a standard floppy disk.
	CD	Optical storage device. Much higher memory capacity than magnetic media, up to 650 Mb. Typically used for the storage of large databases or to distribute interactive teaching material.
	Jaz drive	Jaz cartridges can store up to 2 Gb of data. The cartridges are relatively expensive at around £70 each.
Imaging peripherals	DVD drive scanner	Individual DVD discs can store up to 4.7 Gb of data. Used to convert hard copy material (text and images) into electronic form that can be loaded directly on to a computer.
	Digital camera/video	Takes photographs like a normal camera but allows instant loading of the image on to a computer. The video version takes moving pictures.
Networking devices	Ethernet card	Used to allow connection of a machine to a university network.
	Modem	With a commercial Internet Service Provider a modem is the only option for such connectivity. Most new computers in education now come with a modem or ethernet card which allows them to connect to a network (see Chapter 5).
Electronic teaching aids	Data projector	Allows projection of whatever is on a computer screen in a lecture room or theatre.
	LCD panel	As above but is used in conjunction with a powerful overhead projector.
	Electronic whiteboard	Permits a lecturer to interact with a computer via a standard-looking whiteboard.

Portable and palm top computers Portable computers come in two sizes. The more commonly used laptop computer runs in a similar way to a standard desktop computer. They are indispensable for those who need to travel and perhaps deliver Powerpoint presentations (see Chapter 4) at a different location. It is now possible to get thin, light laptops with a computing power equivalent to present-day, middle-of-the-range desktop computers. Laptops always tend to lag behind the development of desktops in terms of speed and performance, but it is fair to say that modern laptops will all run standard software at acceptable speeds. In addition to enabling mobility in terms of presentations, laptops can now easily be equipped with a credit card sized modem, thus permitting access to the Internet and e-mail whilst travelling.

In recent years palm top computers have emerged. They are small enough to fit comfortably into a jacket pocket or briefcase. Palm tops, such as those manufactured by Hewlett Packard, run a Windows-type operating system called Windows CE. This permits the use of cut-down versions of word processing and spreadsheet applications. Palm top computers can also accept credit card sized modems and can therefore be used to send and receive e-mail. A drawback with palm top computers is that the built-in batteries can require frequent recharging. In addition, the keyboards can be a challenge to anyone who does not have small hands. Palm top computers can usually be physically connected to a desktop computer so that data transfer can occur.

Coping with a computer Computers are great when they work perfectly. They become frustrating when, for example, the screen freezes or the printer fails to respond to the print command.

Most computer reliability issues do not involve a hardware breakdown but are caused by the user inadvertently changing machine settings that they don't know anything about. Alternatively, a user can load software on to a computer that subsequently causes a problem by conflicting with something already loaded. These days, the major inconvenience any PC causes is the occasional freezing of the screen (a crash). This can normally be solved by rebooting the machine, often by pressing the Ctrl, Alt and Del keys at the same time. In fact, rebooting an apparently malfunctioning modern computer often solves the problem that is being experienced. When rebooting, however, it is important to do so properly by following an established procedure (such as Ctrl, Alt and Del). Simply turning the power on and off, which is temptingly easy, can exacerbate the difficulties being encountered, can damage the hard disk and can mean that valuable data is lost. If a controlled reboot does not solve the problem, then it is usually time to consult the experts before uninformed changes are made to the computer's system settings. If, for whatever reason, real experts are not available, then an alternative place to go for support is the Internet and particularly the Microsoft support site at *www.eu.microsoft.com/uk*. Although the first page encountered is fairly confusing, clicking on the support tab at the top right hand corner leads to a page that in turn has a link to the Personal Support Centre. From here it is possible to pose questions related to the problem that is being experienced and be given a possible solution.

Inevitably, computers will sometimes fail and when they do it is often hard, or indeed impossible, to rescue data. It is therefore vital that back-up copies of data are kept. The safest solution is to make copies of key files on floppy disks on a weekly basis. If possible, it is easier to use a Zip or LS120 disk to make back-up copies as this will obviate the need to have several or many floppy disks.

Summary

- The majority of staff in universities and colleges can access a networked desktop computer.
- Most academic staff have a limited knowledge of how easily computers and information technology can be used to support teaching and learning.
- In universities and colleges computers are currently used mainly for e-mail and correspondence.
- All staff should have computers that are matched to their needs.
- There are a range of computer peripherals that are important for maximum exploitation of computers in teaching and learning.

Computer software

The use of computers in education is considered together with packages that permit basic tasks, such as word processing and the maintenance of records (spreadsheet and database software). Some software that is important for electronic communication (e-mail clients and web browsers) are described, as is software used for making electronic slide presentations. Finally, there is a focus on specialised software that can be used in the preparation of on-line learning material and environments. Sources of ready-made electronic learning material are mentioned.

Computers in an educational institution There are a number of functions, directly and indirectly associated with course delivery, which an academic might wish a computer to perform. A list (not necessarily exhaustive) is given in Table 10. It is, of course, very likely that this list will grow in the future to include more of the functions directly associated with teaching and learning activities. Further details of the software listed in Table 10 can be found later in this book.

Table 10   Functions for which computers might be used

Software application	Potential uses
Word processing	Letters, reports, papers, memoranda, timetables, teaching material.
Spreadsheet	Mark lists, statistical analysis of student performance, accounts, graph plotting.
Database	Employer records, student employment statistics, examination question banks, research assessment exercises, subject review statistics.
Desktop publishing	Production of posters, leaflets, newsletters.
Presentation	Production of colour overhead transparencies or electronic presentations.
E-mail	Contacting students and colleagues, rapid distribution of documents, course management, committee/group activities.
Web browser	Surfing the net, downloading software and web pages, e-mail, web page authoring.
Web authoring	Rapid production and publication of www pages, creation and management of web sites.

Getting started with on-line learning   45

Most staff, across all disciplines, would at least expect to be able to produce letters, reports, papers and memoranda. All of these can be achieved to a high standard using any of the better word processing packages (see below). In addition, staff would at some time benefit from using a spreadsheet package to record, collate and analyse marks. It is a big advantage to no longer need to use mark books, where everything is laboriously written in by hand and a calculator is needed to arrive at a final mark. With a spreadsheet package there is little chance of errors in additions and weightings. Using a spreadsheet package also makes it quicker to perform a variety of statistical analyses on the class results. Spreadsheets have a lot going for them during the hectic weeks of examination boards.

Members of staff are becoming keen to produce increasingly interactive multimedia slide presentations. Such presentations can be used effectively in classes in a variety of ways.

A majority of academics now need access to the Internet for e-mail and the www, although e-mail has been a requirement for much longer. It is interesting to observe that most use of the Internet by academics in recent years has been for the support of research, rather than teaching. Over the next few years more academic staff are going to want to be able to produce www pages for use in their teaching and to operate software that allows them to build multimedia into those pages.

Word processing, spreadsheets and databases Word processing remains the most common use for a PC in staff offices, although use of e-mail may well be catching up. Although individuals may have their own favourite package, most modern word processing (WP) packages offer the same range of features, with one of the recent additions (and perhaps the most significant) being the ability to save pages in HTML (hypertext mark-up language) format. This format permits a document to be read by a web browser. Whichever WP package is available in an office, it will offer a bewildering array of features. The likelihood of anyone ever using (or indeed learning to use) all of the features is remote.

The best advice is to learn the minimum needed to carry out the required tasks, at least initially. As long as it is possible to produce desired documents in a reasonable format, it isn't worth trying anything too ambitious. Advanced features should be introduced slowly and incrementally. A new feature of the software should not be tried when an important document needs to be produced to a deadline!

Quite often when a new computer is purchased privately, it arrives with a word processing, spreadsheet and possibly database package. Most computers bought by institutions come with just the basic operating system installed. The institutional/departmental ICT support staff will usually load on copies of other software. If additional software is provided, the same advice given for word processing packages applies. When there is a rush to get marks collated for an exam board, for example, do not consider experimenting with the spreadsheet package.

Web browsers The development of graphical web browsers has been a key factor in the development of the World Wide Web (www). Modern web browser software allows users to point and click a mouse button in order to take a hyperlink from one location on the www to another. It is the user-friendliness of such software that has opened up the information superhighway to anyone.

There are two web browsers that dominate the market, Netscape Navigator and Microsoft Internet Explorer. Both are free and any institution will usually support one or the other. E-mail software is also built into the newer versions of Microsoft Internet Explorer and Netscape Navigator (see overleaf) and some staff may choose to manage their e-mail presence with one of these applications. This should make sense for those who are just beginning to use computers, given that computer operating systems are moving towards closer integration with web browsers.

Some of the most commonly used features of Netscape Navigator are indicated in Figure 2. Note that in Figure 2 the arrow points to the box that contains the universal resource location (URL) of whichever page is currently being displayed by the web browser. Each page has a unique URL, which is essentially a www address that allows the web browser to locate and display the page required. To display any page for which you have the URL, simply type the URL in the location box of the browser and press the return key. Figure 3 illustrates the individual components found in a URL and shows how it is possible for every page on the www to have a unique address.

URL

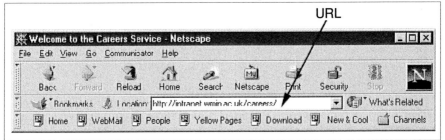

Figure 2   A typical browser – Netscape Navigator
Use the help feature on the computer to explain the function of each button.

Note that in Figure 3 the name of the computer ends with *.ac.uk* because the address is that of a university. Company web sites will end with *.co.uk* or *.com* (i.e. *www.wmin.com* or *www.wmin.co.uk*). It is also worth noting that the first two parts of a URL are largely beyond the control of an individual web author, whereas the directory and filename are not. It is worth trying to keep a URL as short as possible, which means short directory and filenames and as few sub-directories as possible.

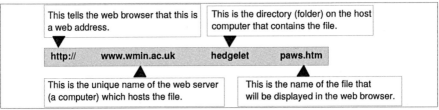

Figure 3   The typical components of a URL

E-mail packages E-mail messages do not go directly from one personal computer to another. Most institutions will have mail servers (dedicated computers) that will receive mail and store the mail until an individual user retrieves that mail using their PC. Equally, there is often a server that will act as a type of sorting office for mail sent by individual users. One thing that the outgoing mail server will do is to check that any mail to be sent from an institution is sent from a PC that is a recognised part of the institutional network. The way in which individual PCs, mail servers and the outside world interact is shown in Figure 4.

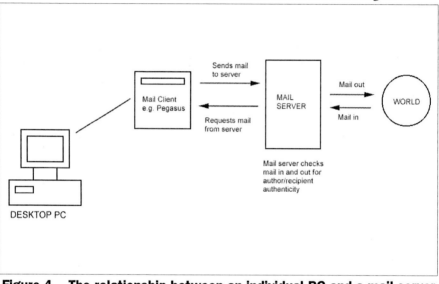

Figure 4   The relationship between an individual PC and a mail server
The user logs on to the mail server using a mail client such as Netscape Communicator. This enables mail that has been received by the mail server to be downloaded to a desktop PC.

For many academic staff, their first experience of e-mail may have been in the terminal emulation software called Telnet. Telnet enables a user to connect to a mail server and retrieve messages. Becoming increasingly significant are user-friendly e-mail packages such as Pegasus, Eudora, Netscape Communicator and Microsoft Outlook. These so-called mail clients do much the same thing as Telnet but all operations are menu driven and there are many features that make handling e-mail straightforward. When the user-friendliness of Telnet is compared with modern e-mail software, e-mail becomes fun to use – even for absolute beginners.

A few years ago attaching files to e-mail tended to be problematic. There was no guarantee that the recipient, who might be using a different e-mail system, would be able to open the attachment. Fortunately, e-mail packages are being standardised in terms of the file format used for attachments. As a consequence, there is now a greater chance that when a document is attached to an e-mail message, the recipients of the message will be able to read the attachment. The facilities of e-mail packages like Netscape Communicator are shown in Figure 5.

Buttons

List of all messages in folder currently selected

List of mailfolders

Contents of message currently selected in list of messages in folder currently selected

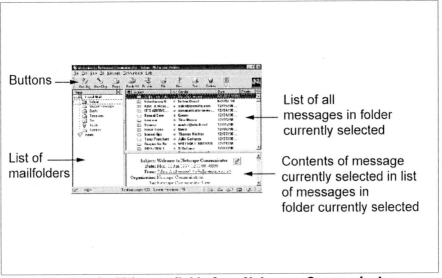

Figure 5   The facilities available from Netscape Communicator

With software like Netscape Communicator, it is possible amongst other things to:

- create folders to store mail messages from particular individuals or groups of individuals
- set up distribution lists so that a message can be sent once to a selected group of people
- filter incoming e-mail automatically into appropriate mail folders
- immediately see whether a message received has any files attached to it
- encrypt any messages sent so that only the recipient, who will have a special electronic key, can read the content of the message
- sort e-mail according to date received
- attach a range of file types to any e-mail message sent
- store messages received for reading at a later time.

Desktop publishing (DTP) and presentation software Two other application types that sometimes form part of a software package arriving with new privately purchased computers are desktop publishing packages (DTP) and presentation software. Most academic staff probably won't need to use a DTP package very often but a few will want to for a variety of reasons. At the top end of the DTP market are Quark Express and Pagemaker. Either one of these would normally be used by marketing departments within universities and colleges or specialised design courses. They are quite expensive, however, and if a modern word processing package is not sufficient for publishing needs, then a much cheaper option is Microsoft Publisher. Publisher is easy to use and readily allows the rapid production of posters, flyers, postcards or newsletters.

Presentation packages like Microsoft Powerpoint help anyone produce effective, colourful and professional-looking presentations. The output can be either an electronic slide show (delivered through a data projector, see Chapter 3) or colour overhead transparencies. Such software is very intuitive.

The basic steps in starting to produce a new presentation with Microsoft® Powerpoint are shown in Figure 6.

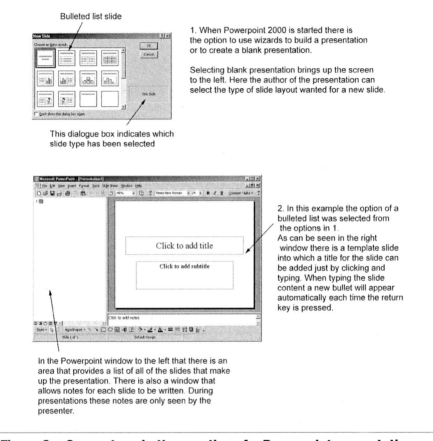

Bulleted list slide

1. When Powerpoint 2000 is started there is the option to use wizards to build a presentation or to create a blank presentation.

Selecting blank presentation brings up the screen to the left. Here the author of the presentation can select the type of slide layout wanted for a new slide.

This dialogue box indicates which slide type has been selected

2. In this example the option of a bulleted list was selected from the options in 1.
As can be seen in the right window there is a template slide into which a title for the slide can be added just by clicking and typing. When typing the slide content a new bullet will appear automatically each time the return key is pressed.

In the Powerpoint window to the left that there is an area that provides a list of all of the slides that make up the presentation. There is also a window that allows notes for each slide to be written. During presentations these notes are only seen by the presenter.

Figure 6   Some steps in the creation of a Powerpoint presentation

Basic materials - text, graphics and layout are assembled on a page. Pages are slotted into a sequence in which they are to be displayed.

*Screenshots of
Microsoft® Powerpoint
reprinted by permission of
Microsoft Corporation.*

Virus protection software It is astonishing to think that people write virus programs with the intention of causing computers, belonging to others, to develop a problem. Such people are, unfortunately, sufficiently numerous to make it sensible to protect any computer against them. Viruses can cause a variety of problems ranging from specific interference with one software package, through to corruption of a hard drive. It is normally necessary to ensure that any computer has some virus protection software installed.

There are a number of such software packages but the three most commonly used are Dr. Solomons (recently taken over by McAfee), McAfee and Norton Utilities. All of these packages scan for viruses in files and can remove detected viruses before they infect further files on a computer. Most institutions will have a policy on virus protection software and a site licence for one or other of the major packages. It is important to set up virus protection software so that it automatically checks for viruses on floppy disks or in e-mail messages. Unfortunately, viruses are prevalent in many institutions even though virus protection software is usually available. The problem is that the protection software needs to be periodically updated (normally now every month) as new viruses are released.

It is vital for individual staff to learn enough about virus protection software to ensure protection for themselves. It is becoming more common for updates to be delivered to individual computers via the www and therefore it should become easier for individual users to become responsible for ensuring the integrity of their own computer and files. In the future, because of the potential seriousness of virus damage, it is likely that institutions will introduce automatic web-based mechanisms for the updating of virus protection software on individual computers.

Web authoring, multimedia and drawing software As stated in Chapter 1, it is possible to get started with on-line learning by using either proprietary or self authored material. So far in this chapter, standard desktop software has been dealt with. There are three specialist kinds of software that need to be mentioned because they are vital in the preparation of basic support and interactive on-line teaching material. These are web authoring/web management tools (e.g. Microsoft Frontpage), multimedia software (e.g. Macromedia Director, Flash 3 or Mediator) and advanced graphics packages (e.g.CorelDraw or Adobe Photoshop). Although currently classed by many as specialist software, growing demand may mean that such packages will join the standard desktop, cost permitting. Software like Adobe Photoshop can be used to create attractive-looking figures or to edit existing images. It is often useful to have an image-editing software package that can be used to change the file format of an image. Images can be created in many different file formats that vary in terms of the quality produced and the size of the image file. Converting the file type of an existing image into another can be necessary for a variety of reasons. Current web browsers can only display images that are in certain formats such as .gif or.jpeg and therefore, if an image file due to go on a web page is in another format, it will need to be converted first. A number of image-editing software packages that save in a wide range of file formats exist. Two of the most common are Paintshop Pro and Equilibrium DeBabilizer (available from *http://www.equilibrium.com*).

The need for web authoring coupled to web site management is forcing an appropriate web authoring package on to many desktops. Web authoring packages are relatively inexpensive compared to drawing and multimedia authoring tools. They permit the word processing of web pages, which most word processing packages allow you to do now with a *'save as html'* option. Web authoring packages such as Microsoft Frontpage or Claris Homepage permit the introduction of a number of active features into web pages without the need for any knowledge of the underlying HTML. Web authoring tools will be discussed in greater detail in Chapter 5. Their significance is such that they are being built into all new operating software (e.g. Windows 98), into web browsers (e.g. Internet Explorer 5 and Netscape Navigator) and new versions of office suites such as Lotus Smartsuite Millennium and Office 2000.

Multimedia authoring software takes the capability to introduce active/interactive elements into material further than web authoring packages. Originally designed to allow production of interactive material on CDs, most multimedia software now comes with a built-in www conversion facility. This allows any material to be viewed in a standard web browser. Multimedia authoring software tends to be quite expensive: for example, Macromedia Director retails at around £500. An excellent, and affordable, package is Mediator which *http://* allows interactive tutorials to be built by non-programmers, *www.matchware.net* using simple menu driven commands. With something like Mediator, professional-looking teaching material suitable for individual, independent learning can be created in a few hours, once a fundamental grasp of the software has been achieved. With Mediator it is possible to drag and drop objects, such as animations, sound and video clips, etc., on to pages and apply events to the objects, so that if you click on one, something happens to another. An educational licence for Mediator costs in the region of £150 and allows creation of a wide range of interactive material.

Web-based learning Learning environment packages enable the production **environments** of organised web-based virtual courses. A number of such software packages now exist and each provides students with a choice of entering various areas of a course, such as the notice-board area or the chat area, as if they had just come through the front doors of an institution. The learning environment is shared by the course tutor, who may be able to set tests, monitor the progress of students or post important messages when they need to. Learning environment software can be commercial, where costs are usually related to the number of students being taught, or can be available at *http://www.webct.com* a lower cost via the output of government-sponsored *http://* development schemes. Two examples of commercially *www.wbtsystems.com* produced packages are WEBCT and TopClass.

WEBCT permits a broad range of activities including:
- student interaction
- monitoring
- assessment
- on-line tutor support
- means of communication between students.

In addition, WEBCT has advanced administrative features that allow student tracking through a course, automatic marking and the generation of overall reports on individual performance.

TopClass:
- provides a virtual environment where classrooms are booked and students are registered for a course
- allows a tutor to provide students with information, create tests and keep a record of student performance
- permits the creation of an on-line virtual community that students can learn to enjoy and use effectively for both individual and peer-assisted learning.

http:// **CoMentor:**
comentor.hud.ac.uk/
- was developed at the University of Huddersfield and is available free to UK higher education institutions
- permits the establishment of learning environments on the www without the need for any additional specialist software
- presents users with four main areas (see Figure 7), the entrance hall, the resources area, the group work area and the individual work area, each area containing different types of tools and material to support student learning
- is aimed at the humanities and social sciences where there is a heavier focus on discussion.

On entering the entrance hall, a student may leave a general message for other students or an administrative enquiry for staff. Once the notice is posted, it can be seen by any user logged on to the system who moves into the entrance hall. In the group work area the course tutor may establish assessed groups and students can set up interest groups. Only members of a group and the tutor can enter any particular assessment group. When a student sets up an interest group, he or she can choose to restrict access. Groups could be used, for

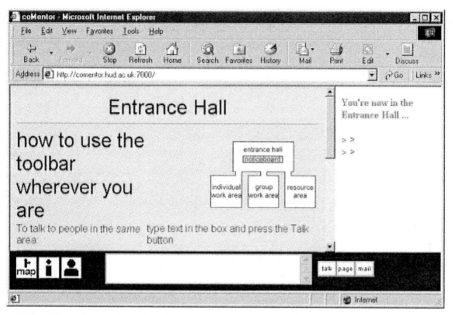

Figure 7   The coMentor homepage

example, to discuss a topic with others prior to the writing of an essay or to develop ideas for a group project.

An excellent summary of the features of several learning environment packages is available from the British Education Communications and Technology Agency (BECTA) web site at *http://ferl.becta.org.uk*. In addition, the BECTA web site provides access to case studies of the use of software like WEBCT, at Havering Sixth Form College as well as Waltham Forest College, Pathway Attain, used successfully at Sutton Coldfield College, and Course Info, used at Halton College.

Proprietary educational teaching and learning materials Ready-to-use computer-based learning material (CBLM) can be purchased but such commercially prepared material would often be excluded on the grounds of cost. In addition, most commercially produced learning material is targeted at the school market and not post-compulsory courses.

Ready-to-use CBLM is, however, available free or at minimal cost via several schemes that have been supported by the HEFCE (Higher Education Funding Council for England). Table 11 provides a summary of the government schemes that have recently been or currently are in operation. The table also gives web addresses where details of the available software can be found.

The HEFCE has recently undertaken an extensive review of CTI and TLTSN. As a consequence of this review, the CTI and TLTSN are to be ended in their present form. In addition, the TLTP programme will be combined with the FDTL and funding from FDTL will only be available on a competitive basis to institutions that have demonstrated high quality in subject review.

Overall, the HEFCE has established a Teaching Quality Enhancement Fund (TQEF). This fund will have three strands; institutional, individual and subject-specific. The subject-specific actions include the establishment of:

- 24 subject centres
- a generic teaching and learning centre (GTLC).

The generic teaching and learning centre will provide support for aspects of teaching and learning that are common to all subject disciplines. Management and co-ordination of the Learning and Teaching Support Network (comprising the subject centres and the GTLC) will be provided on behalf of the funding councils by the Institute for Learning and Teaching.

Table 11   Government schemes

Government scheme	Major features	Addresses
Computers in Teaching Initiative (CTI)	Comprises 24 subject-based centres (see Figure 8). Each centre has a web site with details of software available. There is a news service, a journal called *Active Learning* and a series of primers designed to support staff.	*www.cti.ac.uk*
Teaching and Learning Technology Support Network (TLTSN)	TLTSN activities ended in 1998.* The TLTSN web site is still available and contains numerous case studies on the use of computers in teaching and learning.	*www.tltp.ac. uk/tltsn/ cases.html*
Teaching and Learning Technology Programme (TLTP)	This programme is now in its third phase. The major aim of the programme is to facilitate the take-up of modern technology in teaching and learning. Each project funded by TLTP typically involves several institutions (ranging from 2 to 44) and projects funded cover a wide range of subject-specific and generic topics.	*www.tltp.ac. uk/tltp*
Fund for the Development of Teaching and Learning (FDTL)	This initiative is linking funding to the results of subject review in higher education. Institutions with funding from this initiative will be expected to disseminate good practice across the sector.	*www.fdtl. ac.uk/fdtl*

Note that the HEFCE has recently completed a study into the impact of the TLTSN and CTI. New arrangements for the support of teaching and learning initiatives are outlined in the box on the previous page.

http://www.cti.ac.uk In addition to providing CBLM, the computers in teaching initiative (CTI) also allowed a range of support material to become available, such as case studies on the introduction of ICT into courses and primers on various aspects of ICT. For staff seeking to introduce one or two elements of CBLM into a module, these schemes are certainly a good place to find something. It is worth noting, however, that using CBLM as devised by someone else is often harder than one might at first think. The CTI is in the process of providing a useful, searchable database of material and software available within each of the subject areas represented by a CTI centre (see Figure 8).

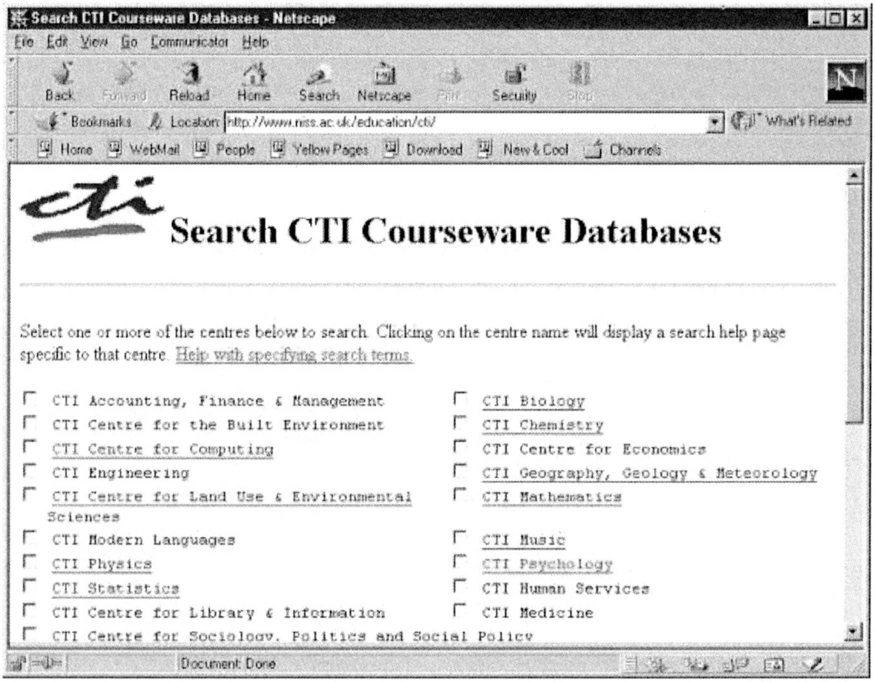

Figure 8   The CTI searchable software databases

Summary

- Academic staff should have software that is matched to their needs.
- Institutions generally provide a standard desktop typically comprising an office suite, e-mail and web browser software.
- Presentations are increasingly being made through data projectors.
- Software that essentially enables the word processing of web pages is now readily available.
- Web-based learning environments permit the controlled delivery of on-line courses via web browsers.
- A number of government-sponsored schemes, such as CTI, have generated both generic and subject-specific computer-based learning material.

The Internet and the World Wide Web

This chapter focuses on the part of the Internet that has most captured the public imagination, the World Wide Web (www). There is a description of how a connection to the Internet is made, either from an institution or from the home. General features of the www are described and there is a brief introduction to HTML, the computer language with which web pages are written. There is some advice on getting started on finding specific information on the www and on writing and publishing web pages.

Five

What is the Internet? The simplest way to picture the Internet is as a very large network of computers that can all communicate with one another, using a common language or protocol called TCP/IP. Thus, via the Internet, Macintosh computer owners can communicate directly with PC owners and vice versa. Computers that are part of the Internet can be personal computers for individual use, or they can be larger computers that act as repositories of the information that personal computer users may wish to access. The larger types of computer are usually known as servers.

http://www.isoc.org/ internet-history/ The Internet was started by the US government in the 1960s as a means to respond more effectively to a nuclear attack. They needed and made a computer network that could provide a rapid response to national emergencies. The significance of the Internet at the time was the fact that it had no control centre. In other words, if any or some of the computers connected to the network broke down or were destroyed, the rest of the network would still function. Some time after, other computer networks from public organisations began to join the system and the Internet gradually grew and is still growing.

Berners-Leigh (1999) Raucci (1995) In 1991 a British academic, Tim Berners-Leigh, was credited with the development of the World Wide Web. Subsequently, the first graphical web browser called MOSAIC became available and suddenly the web began to open its information to anyone. Web usage is now growing at an incredible rate. In 1995 there were estimated to be 14 million regular users of the www. In 1999 that figure was revised to 120 million.

http:// www.commerce.net/

It is easy to think that the Internet and www are the same. In fact, the www is only one part of the Internet. Other features of the Internet, such as sending e-mails, are just as important. The development of the www, with its visually appealing interface, has led to an almost overnight explosion of popular interest in the possibilities afforded by the Internet.

Getting connected to the Internet A connection to the Internet is necessary for access to the www. Sometimes getting connected to the Internet can be straightforward for the beginner; sometimes it can be a nightmare. This depends largely on the circumstances within an institution. For example:

- How good is the network in the institution?
- How good are the desktop computers?
- Does every desk have a computer?
- Is appropriate Internet and e-mail related software readily available?

In ideal circumstances each staff office will have network ports that allow a direct connection to the Internet, via a network (Ethernet) card installed in the computer. Sometimes individual academic staff can have an independent budget that can be used to purchase ICT equipment. In these circumstances it is important to talk to the institution or department ICT service staff before purchasing a computer with a network card. Although most networks can, in theory, accommodate any type of computer, the type of network card used can make a big difference. If the wrong type is installed, problems may arise. If, for whatever reason, an office has no network port, then speaking with ICT support staff is the first step to try and rectify the situation. In circumstances where the lack of a port is beyond their control, either due to the limitations of the network or due to a lack of finance, there are possible alternatives. For example, many institutions now have a dial-up networking facility. Presuming there is a telephone line in the office concerned, a modem installed in the computer would enable a connection to the network to be made.

Connecting to the Internet from the home is normally done using a modem, rather than a network card. Modems are now usually an integral part of modern computers. For the average householder the connection to the Internet is via a commercial Internet service provider (ISP) – of which there are many. As stated previously, academic staff are often lucky enough to have access to an institutional dial-up networking system that works just like an ISP's connection to the Internet. The difference when using an institution's own dial-up service is that there is no monthly fee to pay as there is with the larger ISPs such as America On-Line (AOL) or Compuserve. There are new free ISPs – such as Freeserve and LineOne – where the cost is simply that of a telephone call.

AltaVista have recently decided to provide totally free Internet access for a one off subscription payment of around £30.

http://
www.freeserve.com
http://www.lineone.net

It is worth noting, however, that setting up a computer at home to work with an institution's dial-up system is not necessarily straightforward and usually the instructions provided (if indeed any are provided) are not as 'idiot proof' as those from a commercial ISP. Some institutions are now planning to stop providing their own dial-up service. This is mainly due to the increase in demand for such a service and the appearance of many free ISPs. Although the emergence of free ISPs has been a tremendous boost to Internet accessibility, free providers do not necessarily give a great service, especially when some support is required. For most academic staff, a free ISP is probably adequate, given that some support can always be obtained informally from the institution if required. Using a free ISP to connect to the Internet will normally allow reading of any e-mail messages sent to an individual's institution e-mail address. If you are connected to your institution e-mail account via a free ISP, however, you will not usually be able to send mail from your institution e-mail address. To send mail you would have to use the e-mail address provided by the free ISP. Having two e-mail addresses can become confusing.

Institutional networks and the Joint Academic Network (JANET)

It is quite common for staff within institutions to complain about their institutional network, invariably citing it as the cause of all late e-mails and abortive connections to the www. It is important to remember that the network comprises not only the very small part that is within an institution, but many other interconnected networks across the world. Failures that occur in any office may have little to do with your own institution. Indeed, the average institutional network in the UK is thought to be relatively good, compared to several other leading European states. Most UK universities have, or are working towards, campus networks that link departmental networks (where they exist) to a central computing facility. More frequently now networks are using fibre optic cables to speed connectivity. The central computing service of a college or university normally links in turn to the United Kingdom Joint Academic and Research Network, known as JANET, which is, of course, a major building block of the Internet.

The relationship between different networks within institutions is shown in Chapter 6 Figure 13.

The UK academic community has been remarkably well served by the Joint Academic Network for many years. JANET is connected to several hundred institutions in the UK and is also linked to universities and research institutes across Europe. JANET, through its Internet role, provides the link to the US for the UK academic world. In the last few years the SuperJANET development has received international awards for its transformation of the JANET network from one that carries primarily data to one that can handle video and audio as well. Until recently, the JANET service was free to academic institutions. Due to a shortfall in funding, and in part undoubtedly related to the markedly increased usage in recent years, charges for transatlantic traffic brought into JANET were introduced in August 1998. This is currently at a rate of 2p per megabyte of data. All transatlantic traffic received between 01.00 a.m. and 06.00 a.m. remains free of any charge. *This is good news for night owls!*

http:// www.ukerna.ac.uk/

The www as part of the Internet

Evans (1998)

The World Wide Web (www) has no geographical boundaries and is based on the Hypertext Mark-up Language (HTML). The use of HTML allows users to choose which path to take through an interconnected web of computer files. Web browser software, like Netscape Navigator or Microsoft Internet Explorer, display web pages according to the HTML code contained within them and allow links (hyperlinks) to other documents to be followed. The purpose of a web browser is to allow a user to request an HTML document (web page) from a server and then to display the contents of that document.

The www can be thought of as a massive library of documents, linked together via the hyperlinks referred to previously. One file, on one server, in one country, can have a hyperlink that will take the reader to a related document stored halfway around the globe on another server. This so-called surfing of the www allows one to search for, retrieve and see documents that are stored or filed on any computer connected to the Internet. The documents that make up the www are, however, different from traditional paper-based documents. Www documents can contain sound, video and can also now be displayed in simulated three-dimensional forms. It is also possible to communicate with others over the www, either directly by speaking with them or by sending information via a form displayed in a web browser.

The www is the most popular part of the Internet because it is so easy to access and use. Web browsers are user-friendly in terms of basic functions, permitting even absolute beginners to navigate around the many pages that can make up an individual web site. Usually when you are browsing the web, you only see one page at a time, unless you choose to have more than one copy of your web browser open, in which case you can look at more than one. It is worth pointing out that one web page might equate to several printed pages. Pages on the web do not have page breaks.

These days there are a number of popular things that can be done on or through the web, ranging from shopping to video-conferencing. A variety of helper applications and plug-ins serve to extend the functionality of web browsers, facilitating the expansion of www functions. A helper application will open certain files that web browsers cannot, such as some audio and video clips. When a user follows a hyperlink to a file type that the browser does not directly support, the browser automatically opens the appropriate helper application. A plug-in takes the helper application a stage further by making the file that is not directly supported by the browser appear to be part of the web page. An example of a currently very popular plug-in is Realaudio. This allows a user to listen to real-time audio via the Internet. Plug-ins like Realaudio are often free and can be downloaded from www sites. Examples of plug-ins are shown in Table 12.

Table 12   Examples of plug-ins

Name	Features
QuickTime	This plays various sound and image files including films. It can be used to integrate the files into a web page or opened in its own right as a program.
RealPlayer	This has become the standard for playing video over the web. It can be used for real-time broadcasting. Picture quality can be poor but the advantage of this is that files begin to be played as soon as a computer receives them.
Adobe Acrobat Reader	This is used to read Adobe Acrobat files. Web developers often author pages in this format so that the pages look the same in any browser.
NET2Phone	This is a Netscape plug-in that enables an Internet connection to be used to make telephone calls. With this it is possible to make a telephone call from a computer to another computer on a standard telephone.
Crescendo	Currently the most popular plug-in used to play music files. It enables the use of Internet Explorer or Netscape Navigator as off-line midi hi-fi systems.
VRML	This is essentially used as a viewer allowing the full effect of web pages with virtual reality features to be experienced.
Flash	This is used to display images created in Macromedia Flash. Such images are increasingly used by web designers as they are much smaller in size and can be downloaded more quickly.

Hypertext Mark-up Language (HTML) The Hypertext Mark-up Language was developed in Switzerland by the CERN research laboratory. With HTML a web page author can save text, images, video and sound as a text-only document. Such text files (referred to as ASCII files) can be interpreted by web browsers that will display the page according to the HTML codes used. HTML commands are written as text and are always enclosed by less than (<) and greater than (>) tags. Using HTML, one can specify that there should be a link between some text (or indeed an image) in one document and a part of another document.

As stated previously, web browsers such as Microsoft Internet Explorer and Netscape Navigator recognise a specific HTML tag that is used to specify a hyperlink. The HTML tag surrounds the computer address for the document. That address is known as the Universal Resource Location or URL (see Chapter 4). When a web page is open on a computer, the URL for that page will appear in the window at the top of the page, just below the tool bar (see Figure 9).

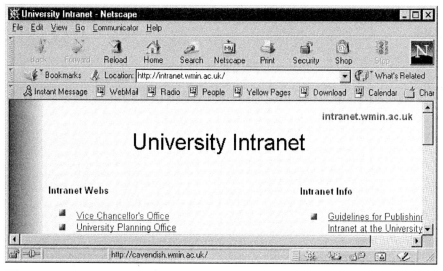

Figure 9   A browser window

HTML has other tags that inform a web browser how to display a particular web page. So, for example, there are unique tags for different types of headings, for tables and for features such as bullet points and numbered lists. An image tag will surround the URL for the image that is to be displayed. Table 13 shows a few examples of basic HTML tags and what they tell a browser to do with the information typed within the tags.

Table 13   Examples of HTML tags used to specify text characteristics

HTML Tag	What the tag tells a browser to do
 	Introduce a line break
<CENTER>	Centre the text
<OL>	Introduce a numbered list
<U>	Underline the text
<STRONG>	Make text bold
<EM>	Italicise text
<P>	New paragraph

For example, to display in a web browser the statement *'The only good computer is a dead computer'*, on a page entitled *'The Academic's View of Information Technology'* the following would need to be typed:

<HTML><HEAD><TITLE>The Academic's View of Information Technology</TITLE>

</HEAD><BODY>
The only good computer is a dead computer
</BODY></HTML>

All tags appear in pairs and surround relevant pieces of text. Note also that the second tag in each pair always has a forward slash as well as the less than and greater than symbols. Every HTML document must have an <HTML> tag, one at the beginning of the page, <HTML> and one at the end </HTML>. In addition, each page is divided into two sections, the head section and the body section, and therefore you can see pairs of <HEAD> and <BODY> tags above. Finally, a web page must have a title tag. Most web pages displayed in a browser have the title of the page on the top border of the page.

This example of a one-line web page, is of course very simple. If the text needs to be displayed in a particular way, then other appropriate tags should be included. To make the line appear in bold text, for example, the following would need to be typed:

<HTML><HEAD><TITLE>The Academic's View of Information Technology</TITLE>

</HEAD><BODY><STRONG>
The only good computer is a dead computer
</STRONG></BODY></HTML>

Each time a new feature is added, such as colour or a specific font, at least one other pair of tags and possibly some words, letters and digits will need to be typed on to the page.

N.B. With the most recent versions of Internet Explorer the browser will in fact display word files in its own window. If a document is typed in a word processing package, such as Microsoft Word 97 or 2000, a web browser would be unable to display that page as seen in the word processing package. The first text would need to be marked up (surrounded by the appropriate HTML tags), identifying the heading for the page, the body of the text and any special features such as bold text, tables or underlined text. These tags can be put into the document manually by typing them in. To do this takes time and also it is necessary to be familiar with all of the required tags. Fortunately, it is now not essential to know HTML to exploit the www in teaching and learning. There are now a number of software packages that put the appropriate tags in place automatically. This means that any page which is word processed can be a web page as well, provided that it can be placed or published on an appropriate server.

As previously mentioned, most recent word processing packages have the option to save a document as an HTML file. This has had advantages and disadvantages. Often when a word processed document is saved as HTML the author will subsequently need to edit the document, as the HTML conversion process leads to changes in some of the formatting contained within the document. The recent release of Microsoft Office 2000 has largely solved this problem. In Office 2000 any word processed document, and indeed any spreadsheet or database, can be saved as web pages if required.

The www as a means of communication There are several reasons for the current focus on ways to make learning more flexible than a traditional timetabled lecture-based course allows in Chapter 1. These reasons include:

- the increasingly diverse student population in terms of:
  - ✓ mixed ability
  - ✓ different learner types and learning styles
  - ✓ maturity
  - ✓ extra curricular circumstances (e.g. parenting or the need to work)
- the increased emphasis on lifelong learning, requiring the need to cater increasingly for updating in the workplace or some form of flexible release from the workplace.

Saunders et al. (1999)
Brooks (1997)
It is clear that the use of technology can promote opportunities for active learning. Advances in technology are and will continue to provide a significant push for change that the academic community cannot ignore. Whilst it is sensible not to allow technology alone to influence pedagogy, we cannot ignore the fact that the way young people learn has been significantly altered by the information technology revolution. Individuals who are now in their forties grew up and learned largely by reading books and listening to people. They would then have gone on to find that further and higher education revolved around these methods of communication. Young people today are growing up with electronic books and interactive games which, despite some misgivings, teach them how to find information in a modern society.

So why is the www so significant in these modern times? The answer lies in the view that the www can be used as a valuable adjunct or indeed a replacement for face-to-face communication. As a means of communication the www offers a number of potential advantages to those involved in education.

Providers of distance learning courses have been giving flexible education for some time, typically combining hard-copy text materials with supporting audio, video and short, intensive periods of student/tutor contact. Many of these providers currently have or are beginning to translate printed material into www pages. The ready accessibility of the www and its continually expanding features combine to make it an attractive option. The www is also relatively cheap. For the provider and students the advantages include:

- fast publishing combined with the need to update only one copy of the material
- reduction in the amount of paper based material needing to be dispatched to students
- facility to combine several media within the one delivery medium
- opportunity for interactive delivery and interaction between student and tutor.

The advantages listed above can impact on all forms of educational delivery. Thus, in addition to true *Some possibilities are* distance learning courses, those which have an open or *discussed further in* independent learning flavour also stand to gain from an *Chapters 7, 8 and 9.* exploration of the possibilities afforded by the www.

Finding information As already indicated, the Internet is a vast network of **on the www** computers and consequently there is a great deal of information contained within it. Finding the right information quickly is obviously key to the effective exploitation of the Internet and www as an information source. Sometimes it is relatively easy to elicit the desired information. For example, finding a university or company web site can be quite straightforward. As the URL for any university in the UK is *www.xyz.ac.uk* (where *xyz* is something you can predict from the name of the university concerned) it can be reasonably easy to predict and type in the correct URL. For example the URL for University College London is *www.ucl.ac.uk*, for University of Kent at Canterbury *www.ukc.ac.uk* and so on. It should be noted, however, that not all universities have three letters representing the institution name in their URL. For example, the URL for Middlesex University is *www.middlesex.ac.uk*. Of course, it is not always possible to predict the right URL (web address) for an organisation, or even for all universities, and so the URL may have to be found in some other way. Probably the commonest (and often fastest) way is to be given the URL by a colleague or to obtain the URL from some hard-copy publicity produced by the organisation concerned.

Finding the correct information becomes harder when a particular topic is being researched and many web sites are being sought. In most public and further or higher education libraries it is possible to search for books on certain topics either by scouring a directory of volumes held (usually grouped into subject categories) or by conducting a computer search of the library stock, using keywords. The www has similar navigation aids to help in finding web pages of relevance to the topic or subject under investigation. Cataloguing the www is a difficult task, however, not just because of the volume of material but because that material is so dynamic. Books in a traditional library will change location only when you pick them up and move them. Web pages are removed completely or change location with one or a few keyboard strokes.

Web directories and search engines

http://www.lycos.co.uk
http://www.yahoo.com

There are a lot of web page directories. Two major ones are called Yahoo and Lycos. Clicking on the search button of a web browser often leads to the opportunity to use one or other of them. Both Yahoo and Lycos are hierarchical directories that function like a telephone directory. For example, within Yahoo there is the general category 'Technology'. Clicking on technology leads to a list of sub-categories including, for example, science and technology. By pursuing sub-categories it should be possible to arrive eventually at the information required. Both Yahoo and Lycos also provide the choice of conducting a keyword search and searches can be customised in a variety of ways. Customising searches can be important in order not to be flooded with possible information sources. Thus, it is possible in both Yahoo and Lycos to limit the number of matches that the search facility will bring to the screen or specify a number of keywords that must all appear in any document selected by the search. Students who conduct a search on the www for the first time are often amazed at how much is retrieved. Whilst the size of the Internet is its strength, it can also be a weakness. Quite apart from the fact that every individual is subject to information overload, there is no control over what is published on the www. It is therefore possible for a search to pick a document that is factually incorrect.

Although the web directories are a good place to start when looking for information, they are generally incomplete and at any one time comprise only a small percentage of the pages on the www. Search engines such as Infoseek and Digital AltaVista don't have directories, but work by searching through comprehensive databases of material on the web. When directory and search engine results are compared for a particular topic, it is usual to find that search engines reveal documents not found by Lycos or Yahoo. With Digital AltaVista it is possible to carry out either form of search. As with the search engines built into Yahoo and Lycos, it is possible to refine search terms. With Digital AltaVista it is possible to limit the search to certain parts of a web page such as the title or the URL.

When using a search engine it is usually best to start with search terms that are as specific as possible, and then become more general if necessary, depending on the number of documents that the search reveals. With most search engines there is usually a help facility with tips on the best ways to carry out a search. Most search engines will respond to some simple commands for limiting a search. For example, enclosing the search terms (the words being used, e.g. the advantages of distance learning) in quotation marks should bring up only documents that have those words in them in the order in which they were typed. Putting hyphens between words brings out documents that have all of the words in them fairly close together, whilst enclosing in brackets will bring up documents containing all of the words but not necessarily in the order in which they were typed.

It is not necessary to use complicated parameters for most searches. A great deal can be achieved by browsing randomly, after carrying out a basic search. There is a keyboard short cut to search that can be used with both of the two major web browsers. A search will be carried out automatically if a minimum of two words are typed in the location box of Netscape Navigator (e.g. fungal biomass) and the return key is pressed. The search result will be returned as a set of hyperlinked documents. If it is essential to search on the basis of one word, then that word should be typed in twice (e.g. biomass biomass). With Internet Explorer the process is slightly different. The word 'find' must be typed before the search terms, i.e. find fungal biomass or find biomass. Because of the interlinked nature of the www, once one or two relevant sites have been found, they will invariably lead to many more sites than most people can reasonably cope with. The incredible number of documents revealed by a search can be irritating, especially if the purpose of the search is very specific (for example, to find out what is the capital of Peru). For questions like this a good web site to turn to is *www.askjeeves.com*. For a detailed list of www search engines and further help and advice on how to use them go to *http://www.niss.ac.uk/lis/search-engines.html*.

Figure 10   The NISS Education homepage

Directories for the academic community

http://www.bubl.ac.uk/
http://www.niss.ac.uk/

Two useful Internet resources are maintained for the academic community – the National Information on Software and Services (NISS) and the Bulletin Board for Libraries (BUBL). Both of these have subject categories with search facilities and links to international services and resources. NISS works with other public and private organisations to improve the scope of on-line information available to universities and colleges. For example, if an institution has subscribed to the appropriate service, staff can access on-line news from the industry and business world and search through indices of news articles and periodicals. To show the services and information that can be accessed via NISS Figure 10 indicates the hyperlinks present on the NISS education homepage. Table 14 shows findings made by following the main links from the NISS homepage.

Table 14   Links from the NISS homepage and examples of the information available

Link from NISS homepage	Examples of information
Administration	University prospectuses; QAA reports; funding and support for further and higher education; support for those with disabilities or special needs.
Colleges and universities	Links to institution web sites; on-line library catalogues; links to institutional computing services.
Common room	Newspapers and magazines; news by area of interest; business and financial news; weather; NISS vacancies service; press releases; details of conferences and events.
Lecture theatre	NISS directory of networked resources (organised by subject disciplines).
Library and information services	Search engines; network directories from around the world; dictionaries and thesauri; learning technology support.
Students' Union	British Council education virtual campus; directory of student media sites; student magazine; Student World UK.
Wider world	News; professional bodies and associations; bookshops and publishers; museums and galleries; travel.

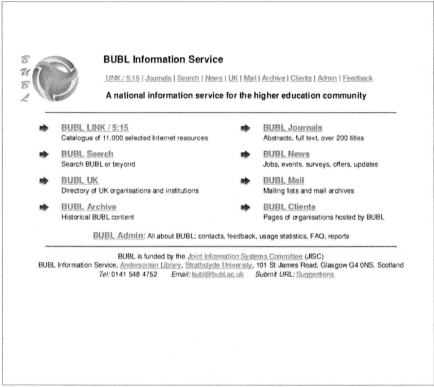

Figure 11   The BUBL Information Service

BUBL is a national information service for further and higher education. The BUBL site provides access to over 11,000 internet resources which collectively cover all academic areas. There is also a comprehensive directory of UK organisations including political parties, schools, museums, libraries and hospitals. One of the major features of the BUBL site, however, is the journals section which provides links to the contents, abstracts or full text of over 200 journals and newsletters.

Writing and publishing web pages

As stated earlier, web pages need to be written in hypertext mark-up language (HTML). An example of how a web page looks in a) a web browser and b) to the web page author, is shown in Figure 12 (overleaf). To write the HTML codes needed to display the page as in Figure 12 takes time, especially without a thorough knowledge of HTML code.

For beginners, and indeed for the experienced, there are a number of web authoring packages that allow web pages to be word processed. In addition, the better packages allow the incorporation of images, audio, video and most other file types of use into the web page created. This is fortunate, allowing the wealth of academically based information that exists in the form of notes/handouts to be readily converted into an electronic form that permits ready access by many people. As discussed earlier, recent versions of most word processing software (e.g. Word 6.0 and Word 7.0) also have the facility to save files as HTML documents, whilst new generation office suites have web authoring tools built into them (e.g. Lotus Smartsuite Millennium and Office 2000). Indeed, most operating systems (such as Windows 98) and new office software suites are increasing the degree to which operation of a computer is integrated with the www. It is increasingly likely therefore that the provision of web authoring and publishing tools, as a standard feature of more general systems and application software, will become the norm.

Romer and Swanson (1999)

Several web authoring tools of utility are freely available shareware or come built into other software packages such as Netscape Communicator. Within Communicator, Netscape Composer allows web pages to be typed and provides a wide choice of fonts, colours and the usual array of font formats (e.g. bold, underline, italic).

With Netscape Composer it is also possible to insert images, hyperlinks and there is a user-friendly publish command and process. In addition, Netscape Composer allows the editing of a page that is being browsed and the dragging and dropping of hyperlinks from a web page open in a browser into a Composer page. It is worth noting that, although it is possible to edit any web page open in the browser in Composer, such editing does not directly change the composition of that web page at its server location. With other authoring packages, such as Frontpage or Dreamweaver, this is possible.

There are currently quite a considerable number of stand alone software packages that, to varying degrees, allow the creation and publication of web sites or web pages. Such packages allow more to be done than freeware packages. For example, the addition of active/ interactive elements, such as animations or forms, is easily possible without any knowledge of HTML.

At the present time, web authoring/publishing tools can be broadly divided into three types. One sort are WYSIWYG (what you see is what you get) editors

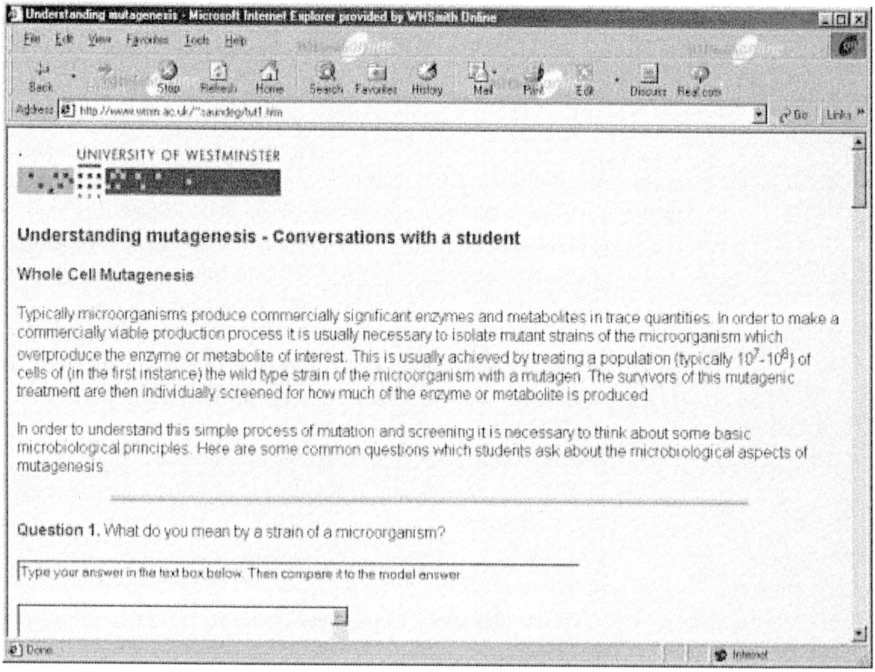

Figure 12a   A web page

where the user is not expected to know any HTML and consequently it is not possible to view any page with the HTML codes visible as in Figure 12b. An example of such a package is Drumbeat, which presents the user with an interface that resembles a desktop publishing environment. Programs such as Drumbeat can become a problem, if it becomes necessary at any stage to change the generally complex HTML codes that are generated.

The second type of package comprises those that allow the user to work in pure HTML code. This is the sort of user environment that is designed for individuals who are used to entering all of the necessary HTML tags for a page manually, via a keyboard. With software

```
tut1[1] - Notepad                                                    _ □ x
File  Edit  Search  Help
<!--This File created 22:17  19/09/97 by Claris Home Page version 2.0-->
<HTML>
<HEAD>
    <TITLE>Understanding mutagenesis</TITLE>
    <META NAME=GENERATOR CONTENT="Claris Home Page 2.0">
    <X-SAS-WINDOW TOP=36 BOTTOM=380 LEFT=23 RIGHT=669>
</HEAD>
<BODY>
<FORM action="" method="POST">

<H3><B><FONT FACE="Arial" COLOR="#AF0000"><A NAME="top"></A><IMG
SRC="images/LOGO.GIF" WIDTH=276 HEIGHT=60 X-SAS-UseImageWidth
X-SAS-UseImageHeight ALIGN=bottom></FONT></B></H3>

<H3><B><FONT FACE="Arial" COLOR="#AF0000">Understanding mutagenesis -
Conversations with a student</FONT></B></H3>

<P><B><FONT FACE="Arial" COLOR="#AF0000">Whole Cell
Mutagenesis</FONT></B></P>

<P><FONT FACE="Arial">Typically microorganisms produce commercially
significant enzymes and metabolites in trace quantities. In order to
make a commercially viable production process it is usually necessary
to isolate mutant strains of the microorganism which overproduce the
enzyme or metabolite of interest. This is usually achieved by
treating a population (typically 10</FONT><SUP><FONT
FACE="Arial">7</FONT></SUP><FONT FACE="Arial">-10</FONT><SUP><FONT
FACE="Arial">8</FONT></SUP><FONT FACE="Arial">) of cells of (in the
first instance) the wild type strain of the microorganism with a
mutagen. The survivors of this mutagenic treatment are then
individually screened for how much of the enzyme or metabolite is
produced.</FONT></P>
```

Figure 12b   The HTML coding required to display a web page in a web browser

like Homesite or Hotdog Professional the author works directly with HTML tags but the software provides various wizards and short cuts that reduce the need for manual coding. For the seasoned web author this kind of software is the usual choice, mainly because no alteration in the HTML coding occurs when you import pre-existing HTML documents. Some academic staff still refuse to use authoring tools, believing that the only way to generate a web page is via manual input of the necessary HTML tags. It is a fact that even the most experienced web page producers in commerce and industry are turning to the use of web authoring tools where appropriate. This makes sense, especially for the academic community, where there is already a tremendous volume of intellectual output that needs to be converted to electronic form. Clearly, to undertake such a massive conversion using conventional manual HTML coding would be impossible from a resource point of view.

The third type of web authoring tool available is a cross between the two referred to above. Known sometimes as compound editors, such packages allow WYSIWYG operations but include the facility to change and add to the HTML code generated. In common with the true WYSIWYG editors, the majority of compound editors do not allow complete control over the HTML code that goes on to any page. This is true even when you import an existing HTML document. The introduction of extra code by the editor can cause minor problems on occasion, as different web browsers may interpret the code put in by the WYSIWYG editors in slightly different ways. An early exception to this manufacturer customisation of HTML was the fairly new Macromedia Dreamweaver, which exports HTML code in exactly the form that it is imported.

Polonsky and Lehto (1999)   The business and academic markets are currently dominated by Microsoft Frontpage. This compound editor is a sound choice, giving a fair balance between WYSIWYG editing and the ability to incorporate additional HTML. A criticism of Frontpage has been related to the extra and sometimes apparently unnecessary HTML that the editor includes in pages that are generated. In addition, some of the built-in active elements of Frontpage 98, such as the scrolling marquee feature, only function in Microsoft Internet Explorer and not Netscape Navigator. In reality, however, these minor incompatibilities are not severe impediments to those wishing or needing to build and manage a large web site quickly and effectively. Indeed, the new version, Frontpage 2000, has addressed and corrected many of these irritations. Microsoft Frontpage certainly provides a user-friendly interface that rapidly and easily allows the creation of many pages with a consistent and professional look. It has excellent web site management tools that facilitate interaction with the server on which the pages are stored. A particularly interesting feature of Frontpage is that which allows direct editing of material that has been published on a server (see Table

PC Magazine 20.1.98 15 overleaf). In a 1998 review of web authoring packages, *PC Magazine* named Frontpage as the premier WYSIWYG editor *'that saves you time with its graphical representation and management of your web site'*. The same article also noted the recent emergence of Macromedia Dreamweaver as a package with many useful advanced features and highlighted the existence of freeware authoring tools, specifically citing AOLpress 2.0 as a package that *'acts like a hundred dollar page editor and site manager but costs nothing'*. Especially useful features of Frontpage include form building that readily allows the processing of information submitted on-line. Macromedia Dreamweaver also has many of these and other advanced features, but it can appear complex to the relative beginner and is more expensive than Frontpage. An educational licence for Frontpage currently costs £42 whilst Dreamweaver retails at around £300. The important features of a free web authoring tool, Netscape Composer, are compared to those of Microsoft Frontpage in Table 15.

**Table 15   Comparison of features in a free web authoring package
with a commercially available package**

Web authoring tool	Features
Netscape Composer	Can word process web pages; easy to introduce tables, insert images, add hyperlinks; able if desired to add additional 'raw HTML' tags; there are template pages accessible from the Netscape Internet site.
Microsoft Frontpage	All of the above but in addition: has WYSIWYG form building functions allowing easy on-line receipt of information from users; has extensive web site management tools with familiar graphical representations of your web site; checks and verifies all hyperlinks in a web site; automatically inserts hyperlinks between pages in a site according to a navigation structure built up in an easy-to-use drag and drop window; has a built-in image editor; allows direct editing of files on the server meaning that, once you save any changes you make, they are instantly viewable to the outside world; facilitates web site management at the server end.

Publishing web pages A few years ago publishing web pages, which involves interacting with a server, could be a traumatic experience. To the beginner, this aspect of producing web material can be quite nerve-racking. In the days when publication relied on UNIX commands (largely incomprehensible to anyone not a computer scientist) things could certainly get very frustrating. Nowadays, however, those dreaded UNIX commands are cleverly hidden behind a user-friendly Windows-type interface that allows non-computer scientists to intuitively follow a straightforward process for depositing their web pages on to a server for all to use.

Publishing web pages currently relies in the main on File Transfer Protocol (FTP). This allows the copying of files from a desktop computer to a remote computer that has a web server on it. To FTP from a desktop computer to a server, the address of the server and usually a user name and password are required.

http:// *www.cuteftp.com/* Modern FTP packages such as CuteFTP, present an environment that is similar to that of File Manager or Windows Explorer. With CuteFTP the user sees a graphical representation of files on both of the computers involved in the file transfer. Files from the desktop computer can be uploaded to the server by dragging and dropping.

Publishing web pages is likely to get easier in the future. As stated previously, Windows 98 has a web publication aid as has the recently released Office 2000 suite from Microsoft. Frontpage has a built-in publishing facility that facilitates connection to a server and subsequent uploading of files. In addition, so-called active web pages can automatically update their content according to information contained within a database to which they are linked. This means in the future that staff may simply need to know how to place their text, images, videos, sound files, etc., into a database that automatically feeds a set of web pages. Since it is possible to have a browser interface with the database, web authoring could become very straightforward indeed.

Summary

- The Internet is a large computer network.
- The www is one feature of the Internet.
- Web pages are written in a computer language called Hypertext Mark-up Language (HTML).
- The www is an excellent means of communicating with others.
- Writing and publishing web pages can now be done without any knowledge of HTML.

Intranets

Six

This chapter continues to explore the technology that underpins the www, outlining some of the advantages that can be gained by the establishment and use of an intranet. The major differences between the Internet and an intranet are explained and there is a brief description of how an intranet relates to the Internet and other computer networks. The use and advantages of an intranet for fast publishing, course delivery and information management are described.

Computer networks

Computer networks have for some time now made a significant impact on the way any business is conducted. Separate networks (often referred to as Local Area Networks or LANs) often have difficulties communicating with one another. This is because networks can use different protocols or languages to enable communication between computers. Effective integration and distribution of information becomes complicated in circumstances where departments have different LANs. This situation serves to stimulate the *Greer (1998)* 'paper first culture'.

This problem of incompatibility can be overcome by the use of intranet technologies. Intranets use a common protocol to share information amongst users. This is the best way to keep key business information (e.g. teaching and learning materials) up to date and accessible. Intranets also have other advantages over LANs. For example, an intranet can be scaled up relatively easily and, compared to other types of network, does not normally cost as much to set up, especially in institutions that are already networked.

Intranets use the same technology and principles as the Internet. Servers are used to store files in HTML that can be read using a web browser. Links can be followed from one intranet page to others and an intranet site can be interrogated using search engines to find documents of relevance. Documents on an intranet can contain all of the same multimedia elements, such as images, video and audio, as web pages found on the Internet. Whilst the Internet is a freely accessible network of computers that spans the continents, however, an intranet network is local, seldom extending beyond the walls of a single institution or building. This enables staff to publish material, comfortable in the knowledge that it will not be accessible to anyone who is not a student of the institution. Figure 13 illustrates how a single PC may be linked to other computers within the same department or the same institution. In addition, it shows how an intranet can relate to the world at large (the Internet) and to partner organisations.

Intranets have been in existence in higher and further education for quite a time. They were usually created within and used only by computer science departments and/or the central information/computing centre or equivalent. Now that computers and networks have become generic tools that other academic disciplines can and should benefit from, it has become increasingly important to open up the use of intranets. Academic departments of all types have started to realise the potential of offering information privately to their own students. A number of factors have contributed to this realisation. One is the growing focus on the use of ICT in the delivery of learning, a use of the microchip that is quite distinct from its use in the education and training of future computer scientists or technologists. Another contributory factor is the way in which modern software for writing web-based material, coupled to user-friendly server operating systems, continues to demystify the whole process of web technology and its use. There is a growing feeling, that, if a college or university doesn't have an intranet, then it can't be serious about the future use of networks. As many commercial organisations have found, using an intranet for information exchange and the management of information can have profound effects on performance. Some of the compelling reasons for choosing to establish an intranet are shown in Table 16.

Table 16   Potential advantages of an intranet

- Information becomes easier to access
- Information becomes available to all who want it
- Users can choose the information that they want
- Information can be published and disseminated quickly
- Authors can constantly update/correct information when necessary
- Facilitates a devolved management style
- Information can be accessed from remote locations
- Allows cost-effective management of information
- Easy and secure storage of large amounts of information
- Paper-based interactions can become electronic
- A new sense of community can be achieved in a multi-campus institution

Establishing an intranet   Physically establishing an intranet can be done in more than one way. Some institutions choose to encircle a part of their Internet server with a firewall (firewall software controls movement between two computer networks or areas of the same network) that prevents individuals from accessing information on that part of the server without permission. To allow private intranet-based interaction with partner institutions requires the development of an extranet, which relies on firewalls coupled to a proxy server to maintain secure communications between the two organisations concerned (see Figure 13).

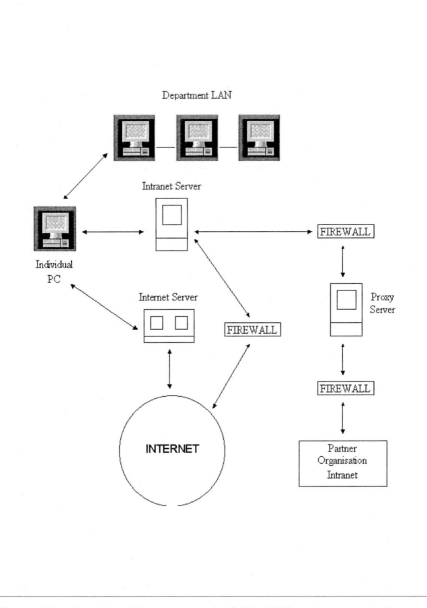

Figure 13   Relationships between individual PCs, departmental networks, an intranet and the www

Intranets in further and higher education Developing and effectively using an intranet can have an impact, if an institution wishes, on many activities in the areas of publishing, course delivery and general information management (see Table 17).

Table 17 Uses for an Intranet within further and higher education

Publishing	Course delivery	Information management
Newsletters Committee minutes Policies Academic regulations Latest news / noticeboard Student services	Support traditional delivery Enhance / develop distance learning courses Facilitate student interaction Staff development	Student records Admissions / enrolment Module / exam registration Finance Personnel services Health and safety

Publishing It is sometimes tempting to believe, if you are an information provider, that sending someone a hard copy means that the job of providing information is done. It is frequently advantageous to adopt this view. The reality is that information provision, if it is to be of any widespread value to users, is a great deal more than this. To be effective, information providers should consider the recipients of the information and what the recipients are likely to do with the information that they receive. There is enormous scope to reduce the amount of paper used in all departments and almost every function within educational institutions. For example, one probably wonders about the value of producing large numbers of paper copies of every single part of documents, like academic regulations, and providing all staff with a copy. Whilst not denying the importance of such a document, it is unsafe to assume that because everyone has a hard copy they will be able to access the information they need when they need it. Equally, it is wrong to assume that any significant message has been communicated simply because everyone has received a hard copy of an important message or notice. The general development of the World Wide Web means increased control for users, who can now determine what information is delivered to their computer desktop. Publishing large volumes (such as academic regulations or financial regulations) on an intranet provides users with the opportunity to choose whether they need a hard copy of all of the information or just relevant parts. Of course, the success of such an approach depends on all staff having adequate access to the intranet material (see Chapter 9). Some examples of the types of documents that have been converted to electronic form at the University of Westminster, with the ultimate intention of reducing hard-copy production, are shown in Table 18.

Once a large document, such as a set of academic regulations, is available in HTML format, it is as easy to edit and update as any word processed document would be. As previously stated, this is as a consequence of the user-friendly HTML authoring packages that are now available (see Chapter 5).

Table 18   Large documents now available on the University of Westminster's intranet

University document	Department/unit involved
University Strategic Plan	Vice-Chancellor's Office
Academic Regulations	Academic Registrar's Department
Quality Assurance Handbook	
Student Representative's Handbook	
Essential Information for Students	
Financial Regulations	Finance Department
Purchasing Policy	
Staff Handbook	Personnel Department
Health & Safety Policy	
University Telephone and e-mail Directory	Estates and Facilities

It is, of course, not only central sections of a college or university that can benefit from providing information in electronic form. Any academic leading a module or unit today will know how much time is spent on producing administrative information for students. An intranet is an ideal vehicle for dissemination of comprehensive module handbooks containing timetable information, reading lists, laboratory or studio schedules, health and safety information, course work details, sample examination papers, model answers, marking criteria and learning outcomes. With such information accessible to students via an intranet, the need to use paper can be reduced by producing a synopsis of relevant module information in hard copy, rather than the entire module handbook.

Another feature of publishing on an intranet is the speed with which alterations can be made and therefore, in principle, the speed with which changes or amendments can be communicated to users. How many times has the final version of a document been photocopied and distributed, only to find out too late about a rather crucial typographical error or a change in, for example, a timetable? With an electronic document there is only one copy to update and there is no cost for extra copies. Publishing on-line takes less time than paper publishing, there is ultimately less paper to buy and therefore the costs of publishing are reduced.

Course delivery Previous chapters have highlighted the value of the World Wide Web as a means of information delivery and as a viable approach in the delivery of flexible and distance learning. There is no doubt that the use of web technologies for the delivery of distance learning courses *Bates (1995)* is growing rapidly. This is logical since the web offers several advantages over the more traditional means of print-based distance delivery. An earlier chapter has already pointed out that distance learning providers have been quick to seize upon the opportunities for reduced print and postage costs by converting material, where possible, to HTML form. Other vehicles of Computer-based Training (CBT), such as CD-ROMs, are gradually being supplanted by web-based courses that can increasingly incorporate more of the multiple media characteristic of CBT. A major advantage with the move to the use of web technology is the enhanced opportunity for seamless interaction with fellow students and tutors, a feature lacking in 'stand-alone' CBT that is based on the use of CD-ROMs.

One of the major barriers to using the www in teaching is the reluctance of many academic staff to provide their teaching material freely to everyone. This is probably one of those rare times when academic staff and management are in complete agreement. Managers also do not want to make potentially valuable learning material free to all. This is especially so for distance learning courses, where attendance by students at the point of delivery is limited, if not completely unnecessary. Development of an intranet can literally open the floodgates, removing a key barrier to exploitation of the delivery medium of the www. Whatever technological base is used to establish an institutional intranet, it is vital that bona fide students are able to access the intranet easily from locations such as the home or workplace. This is possible using secure password protection and is a vital early consideration in intranet development, if staff are to be persuaded of its value relative to use of the Internet itself.

Some on-line teaching activities benefit in other ways by being conducted on a secure and therefore essentially private intranet. For example, when students use discussion webs (see Chapter 7) it is clear that the freedom of their contributions is related to considerations about the likely audience for their comments. As a consequence, if it is possible to make their discussions private to their own discrete peer group (for example, only students on a particular module or group of modules) then the frequency of use tends to increase. Some disciplines, such as art and design, require that considerable expressive freedom be given to students in relation to course work. In the past this has led to the publication of material on the Internet with the inevitable risk that some publications might inadvertently cause offence or indeed break the law. The use of an intranet for such work is sensible, protecting the interests of both the students and the institution.

Sosabowski et al. At the University of Brighton an extensive study of
(1998) the impact of an intranet on departmental activities has
been undertaken within the Department of Pharmacy.
These researchers have looked at the impact of an
intranet from both staff and student perspectives.
Generally, they found considerable demand from
students for intranet-based resources to help support
their learning. Amongst staff, opinion varied. Almost
universal amongst staff was the view that on-line
intranet-based resources could function as an additional
learning resource, but not as a substitute for lectures or
other forms of staff contact. Similar conclusions have
been reached in investigations at the University of
Westminster. Several case studies of the development
and use of intranets have been published and are
available from the BECTA web site *http://ferl.becta.org.uk/*.
At Oldham College an intranet was established two
years ago, initially by a group of staff who were
particularly enthusiastic about increasing the use of on-
line learning material. The Oldham College intranet is
now a major vehicle for the delivery of teaching and
learning materials and the majority of staff use it.
Similarly, a group of six colleges contributing to the
Heart of England Partnership have jointly developed an
intranet to share and develop learning materials.
Particularly useful case studies about the development
and use of intranets have been produced by Nelson and
Colne College and also City College, Manchester. Both
These case studies are case studies examine a common set of aspects of
all available from intranet development, commenting on aspects such as
http://ferl.becta.org.uk/ benefits, cost and issues of staff development.

Management of Universities and colleges currently use a number of
information customised management information systems for the
keeping of student records and to manage institutional
finances. Within an institution there may also be
discrete software to use for activities such as room
booking, space charging, commercial letting and others
(see Table 19). To be effective, all staff within an
institution, be they managers, teaching or support staff,
require information to be in the right place at the right
time. The needs of academic and support staff are
sometimes quite different from institutional or centre

needs, where the customers are more likely to be the funding councils or auditors than the students. There are many activities included in Table 19 that are connected to the teaching function and assume great importance in the daily life of academic staff delivering classes. The major reason that they assume such importance is the frustration that occurs when they don't seem to work very well. Many staff in institutions will have experienced the frustration of an apparent double room booking, the invoice that is never paid or a P45 arriving unexpectedly, because the system had more than one person with the same surname on it.

Table 19   Activities/departments that may benefit from an intranet

• External/internal purchasing	• Budgets/expenditure
• Asset registers	• Employment records
• Health & safety information	• Salaries
• Staff development	• Catering requests
• Equipment booking	• Student records
• Student marks and progression	• Timetabling
• Room bookings	• Marketing information
• Alumni records	• Research grant income
• Student counselling	• Careers office

Although such systems are now normally computer-based they are often 'user-unfriendly', when compared to Windows-based software, and rely heavily on paper for wide dissemination. The different types of information are also often held in systems that are not compatible with one another, impeding the integrated use of the information. One of the greatest strengths of modern information management is the capability to combine information held in more than one database to produce reports that are accurate and therefore of maximum value. At present there is not only the incompatibility referred to above but also the likelihood that the same information is held more than once in different parts of an institution. There is therefore the danger that two or more different versions of the information will be available at any one time.

It is clearly desirable to have management information systems that are easily updated, readily disseminated, accessible to users, but secure to an appropriate level. One way to achieve this is to use an institution-wide intranet as the focal point for information management. As already pointed out, one major advantage of web-based technology is that a common protocol is used, spanning the platforms of both IBM PC and Macintosh. This essentially means that software and hardware do not get in the way, permitting staff to access data quickly from one accurate source. Placing all of an institution's management information on an intranet will, in theory, allow this and considerably more. For example, financial procedures for the purchasing of materials invariably appear unnecessarily complex to users. It is perfectly possible to have a web-based front end that permits users to submit an order and, with the same click of the mouse button, transmit the order to the relevant supplier and debit the designated account. All of this can be done with appropriate levels of security and authorisation built in.

The availability of an intranet can obviously also impact significantly on the way in which a particular function is performed and how effective a service can be. An example of the use of a university intranet to improve a service for students comes from the Careers Office at the University of Westminster. The Careers Office decided some time ago to offer an employment service (the Student Employment Service or SES) to students of the university who were seeking a maximum of 15 hours of work per week to help support their studies. The service initially relied wholly on paper records but not surprisingly this caused many problems. For example, not only was it necessary to make a number of paper copies in the first place but it was also difficult to rapidly match vacancies to students with the appropriate experience. Many job vacancies were going unfilled because of the difficulty in making appropriate matches in time to contact the student and put them in touch with the relevant employer.

Naturally, due consideration was given to entering student information into a database such as Microsoft Access in order to make matching job requirements to students much easier. Each student who registered, however, submitted a form containing several tens of fields and insufficient human resources were available to enter the data. The Careers Office had also investigated the purchase of custom software that could be used to manage an employment service. The cost of such software amounted to several thousands of pounds.

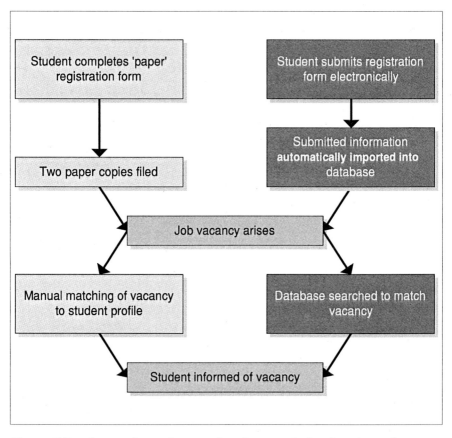

Figure 14   Comparison of manual and computerised systems for Student Employment Services
Note that in the computerised system, two time-consuming steps (entering student profiles into a database and matching profiles to vacancies) have been automated.

At around the same time a university intranet was established. Using the intranet, it was relatively straightforward to set up an electronic version of the paper form that students had to complete in order to register with the SES. This meant that there was no longer any need for paper copies of the registration form. The information submitted by students was stored on the intranet server in a way that enabled it to be imported directly into a database. At first this was done manually by a member of staff in the careers office but it later became possible to integrate the on-line form directly with a database on the server. This meant that the details of students registering on-line were, once submitted, processed by the server and imported automatically into the student employment service database. When a job vacancy arises, staff can immediately search the database to select students with matching profiles and e-mail the students selected with details of the employer concerned. Figure 14 compares the manual procedure for registration with the intranet-based one. The on-line service immediately became very popular with students and over 800 students had registered within the first six weeks of its operation.

Summary

- An intranet can include all of the multimedia normally associated with CD-Roms.
- All types of management information can be shared on an intranet.
- The use of paper can be reduced.
- News/events can be communicated to staff more quickly on an intranet than by conventional paper-based means.
- Intranet access can be restricted.
- An intranet can facilitate a flexible approach to teaching and learning.
- Certain types of teaching and learning activity can benefit directly from an intranet.
- An intranet can be used to automate routine and specialised administrative/support functions.

Seven

Using ICT in teaching

This chapter describes some examples of the use of ICT in course delivery. The focus is deliberately on approaches that are achievable by most academic staff in a typical institution with a functional network. The chapter looks in turn at the value of computers in the preparation of handouts and slides, some of the uses to which e-mail can be put, how web pages can support a flexible learning approach and the potential value of web-based discussion groups. The way in which individual academic staff might gradually introduce increasingly interactive material is also briefly considered.

Progressive development of the use of ICT

A lecturer in further or higher education does not need to be using highly interactive multimedia material to exploit computers in teaching and learning. There are, fortunately, varying degrees to which anyone can become involved in using ICT. The degree to which ICT can influence teaching in a course is shown in Table 20. How far an individual academic takes ICT will possibly be related to the particular institution's teaching and learning strategy. Most institutional strategies identify the possibilities for ICT to support a more flexible or distributed approach. If this is the case, then what can be done by academic staff will depend largely on the current institutional outlook and previous investment in ICT infrastructure and equipment. At the moment, in most traditional institutions, it is possible to go to at least stage 4 in Table 20 by utilising existing equipment and networks. Of course, the ease with which stage 4 is reached will vary from institution to institution and department to department.

Table 20   Levels of influence of ICT in teaching

Stage	Characteristics
ICT Stage 1	Use of computers to produce handouts and overhead transparencies.
ICT Stage 2	Stage 1 and the use of e-mail to regularly communicate course/class-specific information.
ICT Stage 3	The above, plus on-line student discussion forum and electronic slide presentations.
ICT Stage 4	Above, plus on-line subject-specific information resource, such as lecture notes and interactive tutorials.
ICT Stage 5	Above, plus on-line video clips, sound files and submission of course work, on-line assessment, capability to maintain student records, computer conferencing.
ICT Stage 6	The above, plus interactive video-conferencing/ broadcasting.
ICT Stage 7	Virtual learning environment enabling participants to enter a program as a character and experience real life situations.

Preparation of handouts and slide presentations

Most staff currently provide students with word processed material to support classroom sessions that they have produced. The advantage of this basic intervention is that updating of accompanying notes or tutorial exercises can be done without the need (as was the case less than 10 years ago) to throw away the handwritten/drawn original and start all over again. The updating feature of computers is one of their most significant in terms of time saving. An illustration of this is the ease with which presentations can be updated using, for example, Microsoft Powerpoint.

Microsoft Powerpoint

For many years lecturers have used 35 mm slides to help deliver a lecture or support a tutorial session. Updating 35 mm slides has, in the past, required the production of new slides. This is becoming increasingly difficult at universities, as the central units originally established for this purpose gradually disappear. Due to these difficulties, lecturers have turned to the use of overhead transparencies often produced by the process of photocopying diagrams or figures on to acetate sheets. It is worth mentioning that photocopying onto acetate sheets is not without its risks.

With software like Microsoft Powerpoint it is now possible to keep slides in a flexible form, thus allowing easy updating. Powerpoint slides are readily printed on to acetate-like sheets and so, at the very worst, transparencies will be thrown away when material is updated. Printing is not always necessary as slides can often be shown on screen with the aid of a data projector. This means that transparencies need never be produced at all. Instead, slides can be printed in thumbnail form so that students can follow a presentation without the need to copy down what is actually on a slide that is projected on screen. Of course, students can write additional notes on the thumbnail pages they are given. In fact, Microsoft Powerpoint has an option to print a slide presentation as notes pages, which is a combination of small images of the slides with some lines for notes beside them.

A case study from South East Essex College describes the use of Powerpoint to facilitate the training of a large group of students in the use of other software and for the storage of assignment details on servers. This case study highlights the high standard of documents that can be produced from Powerpoint presentations using the built in document wizard. The author of the case *http://ferl.becta.org.uk* study describes how '. . . *Powerpoint also offers you the facility to import pages from other software files and thus provides excellent graphical presentations that can be annotated and labelled.*'

Electronic slide Electronic slide presentations can facilitate some
presentations interaction with an audience. During a slide presentation it is possible to make changes to the content or highlight certain points. Interaction was one unexpected benefit experienced during the delivery of a course using Powerpoint presentations, to a Level 2 group of students in Biosciences at the University of Westminster. It was possible to incorporate suggestions from students into slides, as the presentation progressed. This seemed to have the effect of helping the students to feel part of the teaching session, especially as they were

able to see their contributions displayed to their peers. A factor limiting the widespread use of computers to deliver slide presentations in classes is the need for a data projector as well as computer. There is evidence to show that institutions are increasing the number of such projectors because of demand from academic staff to use this method of delivery. A data projector can also be used to display web pages to a class, thus enabling the use of Internet resources during classroom sessions in traditional lecture rooms or theatres.

http:// www.danware.com An alternative to using a data projector is the use of Net-OP to deliver a presentation directly on to a student's computer screen. One advantage of this is that there is no need to darken the room to make the presentation, but it is, of course, only feasible when all students in a class are in front of a PC (or at most two students per PC). Net-OP School is, however, worth considering not just as an alternative to a data projector. This software permits a tutor to monitor and share any student's PC and send a demonstration into a window on the student's screen, allowing the learner to follow step-by-step instructions when necessary. The software is straightforward to use and provides chat/on-line conferencing modes as well as allowing students to request help by sending a help message to the tutor's screen.

E-mail The use of electronic mail has revolutionised the way academic staff maintain contact with one another. Most institutions are able to provide the majority of their staff with e-mail access. The academic community currently utilises this particular communication medium more for external than internal communication. There is potential within most institutions to increase the use of e-mail for many routine communications with colleagues and students. It is becoming more usual that a student on a course is automatically provided with an e-mail account when they first enrol. In time, students will be surprised if they don't receive e-mail messages from their tutors or module leaders.

Potential uses for e-mail In principle there is a great deal of information that an academic member of staff might wish to provide to a student or a group of students. For example, last-minute timetable changes, room changes or class cancellations are currently difficult to communicate. Often the only way to make students aware of such information is by sticking a note on the door of the classroom involved or possibly the module notice-board. This is obviously not completely satisfactory or easy to arrange, especially for campuses that have distributed sites. Technically, it can be straightforward to establish e-mail distribution lists for each module or indeed each course. Increasingly, institutions will have the facility to generate such lists automatically from their student records system. Despite this, even in establishments where it is possible to generate such lists, e-mail is still used only occasionally to communicate en masse with student cohorts. There are several possible reasons for this, including:

- inability of the e-mail systems to cope with too many distribution lists
- reluctance or inability of staff to use e-mail
- reluctance of students to use e-mail to communicate with staff.

There is a fundamental difference between the second and third points above. Whereas there are still an appreciable number of staff who are not keen to use e-mail, either at all or beyond the basic sending and receipt of messages, most students do, in fact, use e-mail to 'talk' to their friends. They seem, however, to be more reluctant to enter into e-mail conversations with academic staff.

Students' use of e-mail In circumstances where the widespread use of e-mail is problematic, it is probably sensible to offer e-mail to students as an extra way to contact members of staff. The use of e-mail to support the delivery of a module in Biosciences at the University of Westminster has highlighted the reluctance amongst students (over 50%) to use e-mail to contact an academic. The students who took up the opportunity to use e-mail regularly liked doing so for a variety of reasons including:

- the guaranteed certainty of a reply
- the facility to ask questions privately
- the facility to ask questions at any time.

The last two points are closely related and are built-in features of e-mail. Antagonists of e-mail often ask what the advantage of this communication method is over face-to- face or telephone conversations. There are many answers to that question, but perhaps the most important is that it doesn't matter if the intended recipient of a message is not in the office when the student sends an e-mail. Messages received are stored and can be read and replied to the next time the recipient is at his or her desk. In addition, there is no doubt that some students are better able to formulate their questions via an e-mail message than face-to-face with a lecturer. It is noticeable that some of the questions received via e-mail are considerably more thoughtful than those offered in face-to-face sessions. Not only do some students communicate more clearly via e-mail, but their questions often go more deeply into the subject matter.

The use of e-mail in course delivery With the right kind of e-mail system there is clearly scope for much achievement. In the Department of Biology at University College, for example, e-mail is used to enable students to read and appraise essays produced by fellow students. Indeed, there are examples of the use of e-mail for the delivery of an entire module. Using the distribution list and attachment possibilities, *Smith (1997)* Chris Smith at the University of Central Lancashire was able to teach and administer a first year psychology and information technology module. Taken by more than 70 students, there were no timetabled classes and no paper was used for course materials or for the submission of course work. The performance of most students on the module was high. In addition, the module provider was not able to show any link between failure and the delivery mode. Student satisfaction with the method of delivery was also very high. At the City College, *Available from:* Norwich, a course designed to teach staff how to use *http://ferl.becta.org.uk/* e-mail has been devised and delivered via e-mail. The approach has proved to be successful and those responsible are now investigating the use of e-mail to train both staff and students in other topics.

Computer conferencing and discussion groups

Berge (1995)

Computer conferencing allows individuals or groups, around the world or on a local network, to communicate with one another by means of messages on a computer system. Such on-line discussion groups can be a particularly useful adjunct in any type of course in the modern world. Discussion is an important way of consolidating deep learning (see Chapter 1). Most teachers feel that such discussion is most effective when there is face-to-face contact. When such contact is absent or limited, then an electronic means to propose ideas, share experiences and provide answers is undoubtedly the next best thing. Equally, there is much to be gained on traditional courses by employing a combination of face-to-face and electronic discussion.

Staff who have experienced student discussion groups will know that it is not always possible to get the best out of all students in face-to-face sessions. Whatever efforts are made to ensure or encourage otherwise, some students dominate, whilst others make little if any contribution. Even the most able students may not feel as free to say exactly what they think immediately. Everyone has experienced that feeling of '*If only I'd thought to say that at the time.*' Electronic discussion groups provide the opportunity to add to a debate after some thought allowing students with reflective as well as activist learning styles to contribute. There is also evidence that a shy student might use an electronic form of input into a debate happily. This form of discussion can be used in traditional courses as another avenue of communication and learning.

There is more than one way, in a technological sense, to establish an electronically based discussion forum. Standard e-mail has for some time provided opportunities for the establishment of discussion groups. In fact, it is possible to join a worldwide discussion group these days on almost any topic. Several of the more academically oriented groups can and have been used to help provide supporting information for course delivery. The UK has a system called mailbase that supports a wide range of distribution lists. The major problem with distribution lists is that, as a member, you will receive every message submitted by everyone on that list. Newsgroups are somewhat more sophisticated as the user has software

http://www.mailbase.ac.uk

that allows them to download only messages related to a particular topic. Some of the different forms/types of e-mail discussion opportunities, together with their particular features are shown in Table 21.

Table 21   Types of e-mail discussions

Type of e-mail discussion	Characteristics
Mailbase	System established to allow the academic community to set up and use e-mail distribution/circulation lists.
Bulletin boards	These can be used by students to comment on each other's work.
Internet relay chat	This is a form of e-mail where the messages sent are stored in a sequential manner.
Newsgroups	Public discussion groups that can be on almostany topic.

The School of Psychology at the Cardiff University of Wales has reported on the use of Usenet discussion groups to support their students. Articles or messages from students can be posted to one of two newsgroups, one dealing with ICT-related matters and the other for general issues related to the school. An evaluation of the newsgroup service judged that the discussion groups had been successful, based upon the frequency with which the service was used. The evaluation showed that students were more inclined to use the service than staff. A major conclusion was that the success of the approach relied heavily on the extent of training available to staff and students in using the system. With this in mind, the school is planning to provide training in the use of newsgroups for all new students.

Web-based discussion It is quite likely that most academics will be able to find a way within almost any institution to use e-mail to set up a discussion forum. E-mail is visually unattractive, however, and to some extent limited in how much it allows the user to achieve. Whilst it may be fairly straightforward to establish a distribution list, the same will not necessarily be so for a local newsgroup.

In contrast, World Wide Web based discussion groups have several advantages over e-mail based systems including:

- they can be very easy to set up
- they are fairly easy to maintain
- they permit users not only to submit information, but also to search for information
- this discussion forum allows rapid linking to further information sources
- articles can be threaded so that a degree of filing is achievable
- it is possible to control access to the discussion group.

Establishing a discussion web (i.e. actually making it appear in a user's web browser) is not difficult. With good web management and authoring software it can take as little as five minutes to establish a web-based discussion forum with all of the features in the list above.

Use of the forum should therefore be structured as part of a preparation or assessment activity. A discussion web homepage created using Microsoft Frontpage is shown overleaf in Figure 15. Users fill in their name and then submit their comments. New or existing users of the web can search for articles/ comments on a particular topic if they wish.

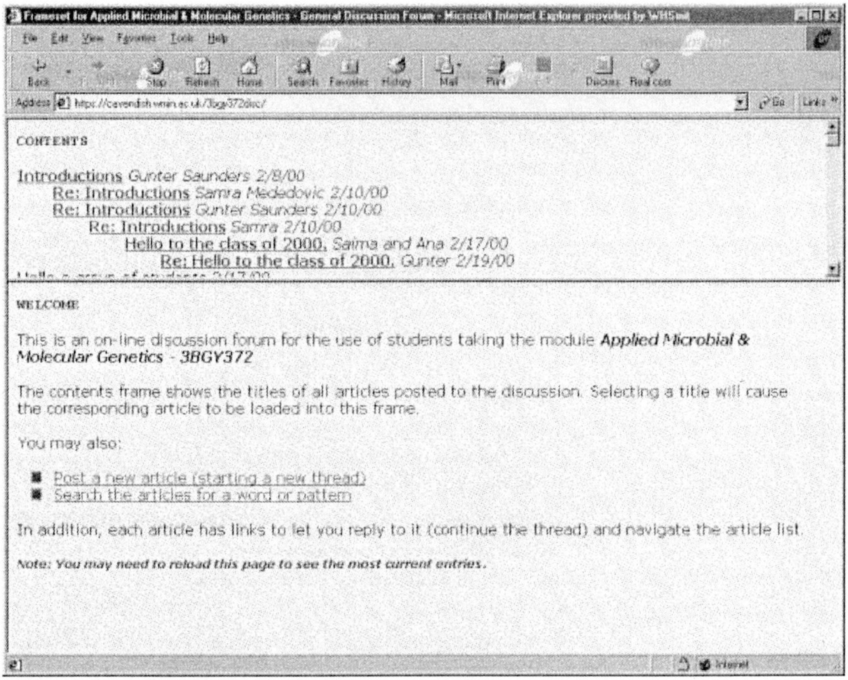

Figure 15   Homepage of a discussion web

The upper frame lists the articles that have been posted to the web site. The lower frame gives users the opportunity to either post a new article or search for articles that have already been posted on a particular subject.

Asynchronous versus synchronous discussion

On-line discussion or computer conferencing can be either asynchronous or synchronous. The former is, as one might expect, currently the most common form and indeed has certain clear advantages. With asynchronous conferencing the participants can access messages and contribute at a time when it suits them. Synchronous or real-time computer conferencing is also possible but the software and hardware demands are greater. Microsoft's Netmeeting is a good way to have face-to-face conversations over the web or to share documents over the web. Netmeeting is included with the recently launched Windows 2000 operating system and provides users with a host of potentially valuable features. Using Netmeeting, tutors can call up the computers on which their students are working and it is then possible to both

http://www.ntu.ac.uk/ vc/vcinfo.html

audio- and video-conference with all participants. In addition, Netmeeting has a whiteboard feature and allows program, file and computer desktop sharing.

A variety of pilot projects have examined the potential value of video-conferencing in course delivery. Several of these have focused on the development of systems of use in geographically isolated areas of the country. For example, Plymouth College has used video-conferencing to provide tutorial support to users of open access centres in the South West that are linked to Plymouth by video. In a report available from the BECTA web site the authors point out that video-conferencing is not a cheap method of delivery, especially if high quality is essential. Other case studies can be found from the *http://ferl.becta.org.uk/* BECTA web site. In addition, the Joint Information Systems Committee (JISC) provides details of video-conferencing projects that have been supported through *http://www.jtap.ac.uk/* its Technology Applications Programme (JTAP).

At the present time, it is relatively easy and inexpensive to buy a small camera that can be positioned on top of a PC, permitting a real-time conversation with someone with a similar camera on another machine in another part of the world. In addition to the camera, software is needed to allow such an interaction to occur. This software mediates the transmission of an image and audio. The most commonly used software of this type is *http://designserver.mae.* called CU-SeeMe, developed at Cornell University and *cornell.edu/cuseeme* free to anyone who wants it. Typically, CU-SeeMe *.html/* connects one computer to another, allowing essentially one-to-one live audio and video. With reflector sites, which work a little bit like a telephone switchboard, it is possible to deliver a multi-participant conference. The limiting factor in video-conferencing at the moment *http://www.ntu.ac.uk/* is bandwidth (the network information capacity). Both *vc/vcinfo.html* participants in a single site to single site conference must have a connection to the Internet or local network that can process a lot of data very quickly as both video and audio files are large. Currently, even if a reflector site is available, only students with high quality modems will be able to see and hear effectively. No one is likely to learn too much from seeing a slow motion lecture! Live, Internet-based video-conferencing will probably have a big impact on teaching and learning in the future, when every student has the means to receive and respond in real time.

Due to the considerable demands on resources (at both staff and student ends) there are currently few, if any, institutions that could claim to be able to use video/audio links for a significant amount of teaching. Video-conferencing, however, will eventually become as usual an activity as making a telephone call. This is inevitable as advances in equipment, such as the development of faster cable-based modems, overcome the current bandwidth problem that prevails at present and limits the widespread use of such technology. Beyond faster modems are broadband connections that are due to be on the market quite shortly. Even the slowest broadband connection will download data at 10 times the speed of current top-range modems. Such download capability makes the availability of live video to a wide number of locations much more feasible. For home users, however, to have the British Telecom broadband service, which is called ADSL, it is estimated that a payment of between £35 and £50 per month will need to be made. It is hard to see how students studying at or from home will be able to afford this without some form of subsidy or until competition drives the price down.

Lecture notes on the web What is the use of simply placing lecture notes on the www? Is this of value to students and staff? Won't it just mean that students will not attend lectures? These questions are commonly asked on courses about the use of the Internet or web technology in teaching and learning. The answer is, of course, that it is of use and valuable to put lecture notes on to the web. They are of value to students who happen to miss lectures and are of enormous benefit to students who would prefer to listen in lectures rather than have to write notes as they listen. Of course, in most cases it is better to have interaction in any material that is computer-based. This, however, can be done gradually at later dates. Putting lecture notes on to the web is a start, a first step in using web technology that nevertheless is useful in its own right.

It is interesting to note that the third question above was also raised after the National Student's Union convinced the teaching profession of the desirability of lecture handouts, back in the 1970s. The worry that students may not attend has not prevented the profession from going handout crazy, much to the annoyance of managements who wish to keep their photocopying bills down! The widespread use of handouts does not appear to have markedly affected student attendance at lectures.

Making material interactive The placing of lecture notes on the www or an intranet is not difficult, although it can take some time. The time it takes to convert existing material composed of text and images is, of course, directly related to the degree that an individual is 'computer literate'. In certain cases, depending upon the type of material involved, it becomes possible to introduce elements of interaction fairly readily. For example, a combination of text and images (common in material normally distributed to students in handouts) allows the introduction of exercises that give a student the opportunity to do something, rather than just read. So, for example, it is possible to have students attempt to summarise something they have read about in the form of a diagram, before following a hyperlink to the diagram itself. Equally, annotated diagrams can be easy to duplicate as separate files without the annotation. Students can then be asked to annotate a printed copy of the diagram according to text-based information within the lecture notes. Most of these efforts to engage students with the on-screen material rely on the students being sufficiently responsible not to jump the links to find the answer, before they try the exercise that they were intended to complete. Naturally, there are electronic ways of preventing students from accessing an answer before completing an exercise. This will often require the intervention of a computer specialist and is therefore beyond the average non-computer scientist who is starting out on the road of on-line learning. There is no easy way around this problem at present except perhaps to choose to be slightly less sceptical than some and believe that students can be made to realise the benefits gained from not just jumping to the answers. An intermediate solution to the potential problem of providing students with all of the answers is to reveal the answers progressively to students on-line, as the course continues. Such web management is possible when modern web authoring software is used.

A relatively straightforward method for providing some means of on-line interaction with a collection of web-based lecture notes is via e-mail. Alternatively, a combination of e-mail, for individuals who wish to communicate with you privately, and a discussion forum (see above) which the whole class uses, can be very effective.

Flexible learning and notes on the web Lecture notes available on the web or on an intranet can be used to promote a flexible learning approach in a traditional setting. An example of this comes from the delivery of a module on Microbial Genetics to students in their second year at the University of Westminster. For this approach the entire taught module content had been converted to web-readable material comprising lecture notes and tutorials. Students were provided with all of the HTML files on a floppy disk to facilitate access for those without a networked computer at home. The lecture notes were liberally sprinkled with diagrams that provided a means to introduce the potential for simple interaction (see above) on the part of the learner. Self assessment exercises designed to test understanding were also built into the material.

The approach taken with this material involved reducing the formal lecturing on the module and replacing it with more discussion-centred sessions. This was done by asking students to use the web-based materials to prepare for classroom sessions. In addition, students were encouraged to use e-mail to pose questions to the lecturer that could be used to help introduce the next classroom topic.

Students' views At first the students involved in the approach described above were quite concerned about the fact that there would be little, if any, formal lecturing. It was relatively easy to persuade them that the approach was worth trying, however, and once they had been able to print off selected copies of the lecture notes they seemed a lot happier! Despite the fact that they did quickly realise that the regular weekly attendance 'carrot' of lecture handouts was not there, attendance at the classroom sessions did not fall off significantly. The exception to this were a few independent learners who only attended the laboratory sessions and the two classroom sessions where attendance was specifically requested by the lecturer. These students normally had significant external commitments, such as the need to work at times that clashed with classes or young children who required care. The opportunity to study the material independently and use e-mail when they needed to contact the lecturer, was an approach that suited them.

Evaluation of web-based material At the end of the semester the success of the approach was measured via extensive student feedback involving questionnaires and structured interviews with students on a one-to-one basis. The major conclusions are given below:

- There was evidence of the value of the approach for independent learners and mature students with family or work commitments.
- There was evidence that the www material was valued and useful as a supplement to support classroom sessions.
- There was evidence of the danger of 'spoon feeding' such that the students only read the www material.
- There was strong support for concentrating attendance on activities, discussions, etc., rather than lectures.
- The majority of respondents found accessibility to the full module content at the start of the semester very useful.
- Most students printed off the on-line material at some stage although appreciable numbers did some work on screen.
- Many students pointed out that the www material was especially useful for revision.

Overall performance was better than in previous years, when a more 'usual' lecturing approach had been adopted. Out of 32 students, four failed the module. The average mark was higher than it had been in the previous six years and it was noticeable that student performance, on short answer question sections of the examination, was much better than usual. The highest mark for the module, 77%, was obtained by one of the students who only attended when strictly required to.

A degree of scorn is sometimes aimed at those who place lecture notes on the web. Making a lot of text accessible through a screen-based interface may be treated with scepticism by those steeped in the development of distance learning courses or interactive multimedia materials (IMM). There is evidence that questions the value of such an approach. A variety of research indicates that individuals are more likely to skim through 'chunks' of text when given on a screen rather than on a printed page. As pointed out previously, however, text-based teaching information does have value to students, especially when used to reinforce and support classroom-based learning. In fact, the value of any approach involving the use of on-line teaching material will always be related to how it is used and how it fits into the overall teaching strategy. That is the case no matter how sophisticated the technology that lies behind its production.

CD-ROMs, interactive multimedia and the learning environment

Another commonly held view amongst academic staff who have little or no experience of the use of computers in teaching is that all valuable on-line learning material comes on a CD-ROM and has incredibly advanced simulation and visualisation aspects. Such truly interactive multimedia (IMM), with moving images, sound, video and the capability of providing the user with a high degree of control over the path that they follow through the material, takes a lot of resource to develop. Consequently, most IMM currently available has been either commercially produced or developed through one or other government-supported scheme at selected institutions. This is despite the existence of many quite user-friendly software packages that allow one to design multimedia teaching material with no programming knowledge at all.

Where such highly interactive material is available, the temptation to use it is strong. There is little doubt that such material will prove attractive to students, leading to (at least momentarily) a raising of their interest in what is being studied. Equally, it is clear that, where such material is used, it can often add an extra dimension to learning, allowing students to break through an otherwise difficult barrier in their path to understanding a topic. It is not always the case, however, that IMM is the best way to teach a particular topic or part of a topic. Having said that, there is clear evidence to show that it is a particularly useful approach when focusing on complex processes that require simulation (e.g. microscopic activities).

For the average academic member of staff seeking to begin an exploration of ways to make teaching and learning more effective or efficient, IMM is something that can only be used sparingly. Leaving aside pedagogical issues for a moment, the time it takes to create IMM material is too great for most lecturers to even think about developing large amounts of their own material. Certainly, where an inexpensive piece of IMM is available, it is worth considering including it in a course to support whatever topic it addresses, if only to add a further learning approach that could be important in increasing the subject understanding of some students. Otherwise, a slow incremental approach to the addition of IMM in a course is advisable.

Software that permits the establishment of electronic learning environments has been described in Chapter 4. Whether an individual member of staff is able to make use of such software will depend on the circumstances within their institution. Commercial learning environment software is not cheap. To take learning environment software and start using it requires someone to have the time to understand how the software works. It is unlikely that most academic staff, especially if they are relative novices with on-line learning, will be able to find sufficient time. Consequently, the implementation of a learning environment package may well depend on whether there is a member of the central or local computing support staff who is able and willing to help set it up. If there is such a person, possibly steered by an institution policy in the use of learning environments, then they are undoubtedly worth investigating. It can, however, be easier and cheaper to build a learning environment from available institutional resources such as the e-mail system, combined with an intranet or the Internet and web authoring software.

Summary

- There are a number of levels at which one can introduce the use of computers into teaching.
- Presentation software is valuable for the periodic updating and correction of slides.
- Electronic slide presentations can allow interaction with students during classroom sessions.
- E-mail is a fast-growing means to communicate with the diverse student population of today.
- Students are very positive about the use of e-mail.
- Computer conferencing, especially via web-based discussion groups, offers opportunities for deep learning to occur.
- A degree of interaction can be readily incorporated into web-based lecture notes.
- The use of web-based notes can support a flexible learning approach.
- Students are generally positive about the value of web-based resources.
- Producing interactive multimedia takes considerable time.
- A progressive approach to the development and use of computer-based materials in teaching is recommended.

On-line assessment

This chapter focuses on the major issue of assessment and tries to show how computers and appropriate software can be used to reduce the assessment burden faced by academic staff. The types of questions that can be marked automatically are described. There is a detailed description of one commercial testing package that is particularly user-friendly and provides scope for instant feedback. The chapter closes by briefly considering the issue of tracking and recording students' progress.

The purposes of assessment A major pressure that all academics face is to keep up with the increasing burden of assessment of student achievement. Whilst setting assessments is not necessarily a problem, marking them in good time and providing feedback to large numbers of students certainly are. Largely because of this, it is very rare for academic staff to have the time to think too deeply about why they assess the students that they teach. When they find the time, it is often a surprise to realise that assessment can actually be an important tool in effective learning, rather than just the means to decide whether a student gets a pass, a lower second or a first.

Another surprise, perhaps related to the pressures that the system faces, is how many younger staff fail to understand the difference between formative and summative assessments. Almost all staff are exclusively involved in the latter, which enables them to build a portfolio of marks for each student so that end-of-semester decisions about whether someone has passed a module or not can be made. There is no doubt that many staff perceive such summative assessments as a means to help students diagnose any misunderstandings. The majority of students, however, would welcome opportunities to carry out such diagnoses without the added pressure of knowing that marks depend upon it.

There are a number of factors which mean that, to some degree, the formative aspects of assessment, where the emphasis is on allowing a student to understand their weak points on a particular topic, is being lost.

These factors include:
- the growth in the use of course work as a part of the overall summative assessment of student learning
- large classes, which mean that staff can only just manage to provide feedback on required summative assessment leaving little scope or time for purely formative exercises
- student preconceptions that assessments are purely to obtain a mark.

Naturally, some will say that, as formative assessment can comprise a large degree of self assessment, the first two points should not be that significant. Such a view, however, would not be taking into account either the degree to which students are focused on summative assessment or the limited amount of time that staff have to design and subsequently provide support for formative exercises. It is often said that assessment comprises the real curriculum for students and dispelling this view, without totally abandoning assessment or assessing every topic on a course, is very hard.

Assessment types Assessment can be grouped in a variety of ways. An initial division into summative and formative and norm-referenced or criterion-referenced. Norm-referenced assessment (where performance is scored in relation to the average mark obtained by a peer group) is used only infrequently for formative purposes, whereas criterion-based judgements are almost always used for any summative exercises. Beyond this, assessments can be purely objective, as for example with tests that require only factual recall, or they can test so-called higher level skills such as the abilities to analyse and evaluate. It is normal for objective testing to be carried out by using short answer tests, often traditionally of the multiple choice type. That is not to say that short answer tests cannot be used to assess a student's ability to think critically. It is more usual, however, for assessment of higher level skills to be conducted via traditional unseen examinations, normally comprising essay-type questions. It is interesting to note, though, that in many unseen examinations there are usually sufficient numbers of marks available for what is essentially little more than factual recall. Other types of assessment deserve a mention. Both self assessment and peer assessment can be used effectively to help students find out more about their level of understanding of a topic. A variety of group work and reflective practices, such as the keeping of a diary, can also be used to support formative assessment on a course.

In traditional institutions the use of a variety of assessments is generally considered to be a good idea. Whilst there is no doubt that the use of different assessment types e.g. essays, oral presentations, poster presentations serves to help prevent students from becoming bored too quickly, varying assessment type is no use if appropriate high level skill learning outcomes are not tested. Many people take the view that having a variety of assessment exercises automatically means that they are assessing in an innovative manner. In many respects it doesn't matter if all of the assessments that a student undertakes are of more or less the same type, provided that collectively they test knowledge, understanding and the ability to critically evaluate and interpret. All that is really important in the hard-pressed education systems of today is that assessments are chosen so as to challenge students and measure their capabilities whilst generating a manageable workload for those responsible for setting the assessment and providing feedback. This means that it is necessary to examine carefully the purposes of assessments that are currently set. This should be done in order to determine whether less traditional assessment types, that take little time to mark and provide feedback, are fit for the purpose intended. A simple example will illustrate the significance of this. If it were considered important for a history student to know a series of significant dates in world history, then setting an essay (given the time needed to mark essays) does not make sense. Such fundamental fact-based assessment would best be done using a short answer test. The relative ease with which computers can now be used to mark such tests makes it even more sensible to consider how individual assessments are best undertaken.

Computers in assessment Computer-based assessment can mean different things to many people. Academic staff have been using computers to support the assessment process for some time, using a spreadsheet package to help collate and record marks or database software to maintain a bank of examination questions, for example. Computers are also commonly employed to help manage assessment through the use of optical mark readers, which are invaluable in the marking of paper-based multiple choice tests.

For the purposes of this chapter, computer-based assessment is considered to be something that is carried out completely by computer. Ideally, such computer-based assessment will perform a number of tasks in addition to presenting the test questions. Modern, user friendly software would be expected to record and enable analysis of class marks, as well as provide a student taking the test with feedback.

It is still common to encounter a high degree of suspicion on the part of academic staff towards the use of computer-based assessment. This is partly because staff are suspicious of computers but, more significantly, because computer-based testing is often thought to comprise only multiple choice questions. Many consider the multiple choice test a risky form of assessment given the possible influence of guesswork and the failure of such tests to examine adequately anything other than purely objective ability. Two important points should be made. The first is that there is no reason why multiple choice questions cannot be used to examine the capability of a student to think and analyse. In addition, some modern software permits the setting of not only multiple choice questions but also a wide variety of other question types, such as fill in the blanks and multiple response.

Advantages of computer based assessment Computers offer a number of ways to provide assessments that can be formative, summative or both. There are several advantages of using computer-based assessment over paper based equivalents including:

- the speed with which marking can occur
- the capability to incorporate instantaneous feedback
- the possibility of incorporating in depth analysis of student responses
- the opportunity to adapt assessment and learning to individual requirements
- the ability to include multimedia within the assessment environment
- the opportunity to take a formative test more than once
- the potential to link an on-line assessment system to central record keeping and awards.

All academic staff are aware of the time spent marking assessments, therefore any help that computers can give would be welcomed by the majority, as would the capability to provide instantaneous feedback. Beyond this, of course, the opportunity to tailor the questions and feedback provided to individual learning needs is a goal often spoken about but hardly achievable by conventional means, in a mass education system composed of diverse groups of students.

Software that can provide on-line assessment Some basic types of self assessment are easy to provide on-line and can be recommended as a way of making any computer-based material more engaging. Using web technology and authoring software such as Microsoft Frontpage, it is straightforward to set a problem or problems as one web page, whilst the answers are only a mouse click away. In its simplest form this type of assessment provides no feedback, just the answers. Web pages can be as large as necessary, however, and so advice to students who get an answer wrong can also easily be made available on-line. A self assessment produced in this way relies on students having the discipline not to simply click the mouse button to see an answer before they have tried to solve the problem themselves. One way to get around this is to make the answers available to students on-line only when there is some evidence that the questions have been attempted.

There are two common 'low technology' ways to approach this. Some lecturers find that the simplest solution is to phase in the availability of the answers as a course progresses. For those who wish to be more certain that students are not just accessing the answers without trying to solve the problem themselves, it is fairly straightforward to require students to e-mail their efforts prior to release of the correct answers. If a class is very large, however, the latter approach can become difficult to persevere with, and in the long run the advantages of not making answers freely available are outweighed by the disadvantages.

In on-line tests a student is typically provided with a form on screen (see Figure 16) where they can select an answer from a choice or fill in a single response to a question. The example shown in Figure 16 was constructed using basic web authoring software.

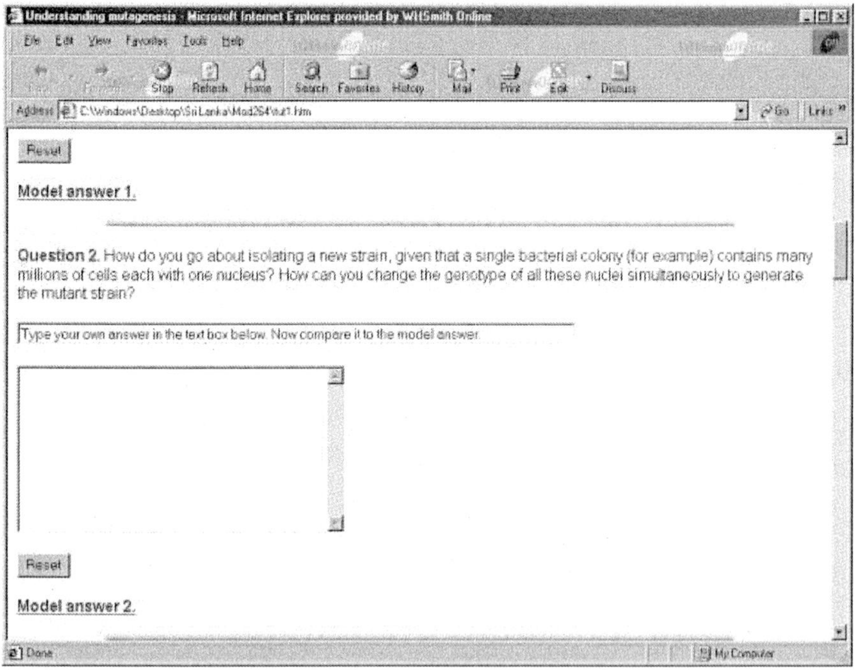

Figure 16   An example of a basic on-line self assessment question
Students can click at any time on the hyperlink to a model answer.

Formative tests can also be prepared using multimedia authoring tools such as Mediator (see Chapter 4). With software like Mediator it is possible to incorporate multimedia into questions so that, for example, a wrong answer provides the student with a pre-programmed message or sound. The message could include a hint to the student enabling them to make an informed second attempt.

Naturally, although self assessment is desirable and can serve to take some load away from staff, systems that can automatically provide feedback and/or mark are likely to have greater impact. With such systems there is clear potential to save time, speed up turn-around time, reduce resources required for the maintenance of records and increase the ease with which data collected can be used. Although all these advantages sound great, it is important to remember that such automated systems generally only cater for the test type of assessment. Currently, there is no widely available software that will mark and give feedback on more subjective assignments, such as essays. Having said that, there are some emerging examples of software designed to streamline the process of marking and feeding back on more subjective forms of assignment. Typically, such software facilitates the provision of standard 'chunks' of feedback and advice to students, according to deficiencies identified by the marker. Another example of software used to correct assignments is the Ceilidh system which was developed at the University of Nottingham. This software enables first year students to obtain accurate on-line feedback on the quality of computer code that they have written, removing a load from the shoulders of hard-pressed academic staff.

http://www.mindtrail.com/

http://www.cs.nott.ac.uk/~ceilidh/

There is a great deal more to the test type of assessment software than is apparent at first sight. To begin with, such software is not always, as many might think, restricted just to the setting of multiple choice questions. Among critics of multiple choice, or 'multiple guess' tests as some will refer to them, is the general feeling that such tests do little other than engage the ability of students to memorise facts. This issue, however, is a question of design, and can apply equally to the setting of any other form of assessment, including essays. It is possible to set short answer questions that adequately test higher level skills, such as the capability to bring together a number of sources of knowledge and experience in order to solve a problem. The ability to set such short answer questions is certainly supported by the features inherent in modern commercially available software designed for the purpose of increasing the use of computers for on-line testing.

There are now a number of software packages available specifically for the production of on-line tests. The most frequently encountered commercial software is Q-Mark or Question Mark. This software is available for both PC and Macintosh operating systems and can support a wide variety of question types including multiple choice. In addition, however, Q-Mark allows multiple response, which permits users to select none or more than one from a series of choices and fill in the blanks. Q-Mark also supports text match answers, where a student types in an answer which is then checked against a list of acceptable responses, and hot spots where a student must point at a particular part of a graphic to receive a mark. There are also on-line assessment tools that are freely available to the academic community as a consequence of government-funded development work carried out in universities. For example, the CASTLE project, funded jointly by the Joint Information Systems Committee and JTAP, provides a toolkit that can currently be used to set up and mark multiple choice tests.

http:// www.qmark.com

http://www.le.ac.uk/cc/ ltg/castle/

Tests devised with software such as Question Mark Perception allow feedback to be instantly returned in the form of a mark and/or additional comments. The web-based Q-Mark software is user-friendly to both the originator of the test and users of the test. The software is broadly divided into two parts, the so-called question manager and the session manager. The question manager has a wizard function that guides a lecturer through the steps of setting test questions. Once a question bank has been established in this way it is possible to construct tests by drawing selected questions from the bank using the session manager.

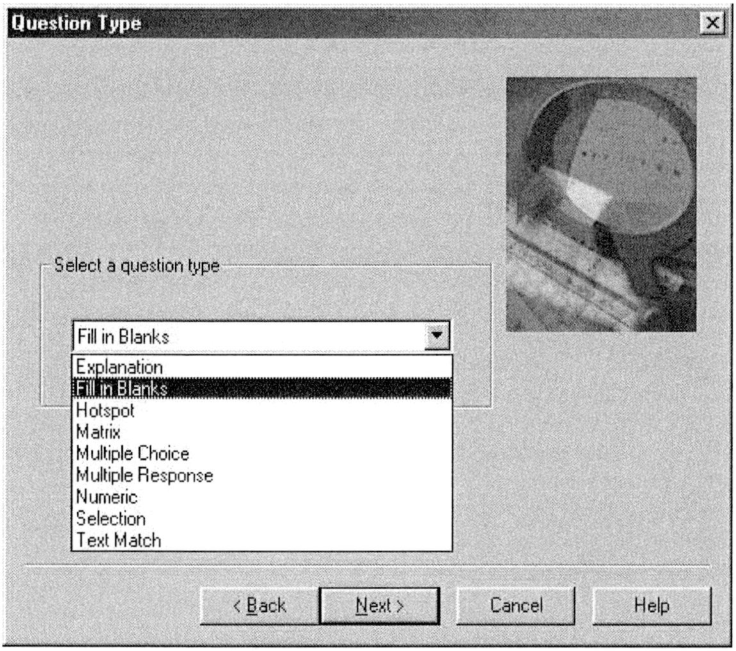

Figure 17   The question manager wizard in Question Mark Perception
Note the capability to select a wide range of question types.

When setting questions, the wizard presents the user with the opportunity to select from a wide range of question types (see Figure 17).

As one progresses through the wizard there is also a chance to provide feedback comments that will be given to students when they have answered the question. An example of a multiple response question is shown in Figure 18. What a student sees, having attempted and answered incorrectly, is shown in Figure 19.

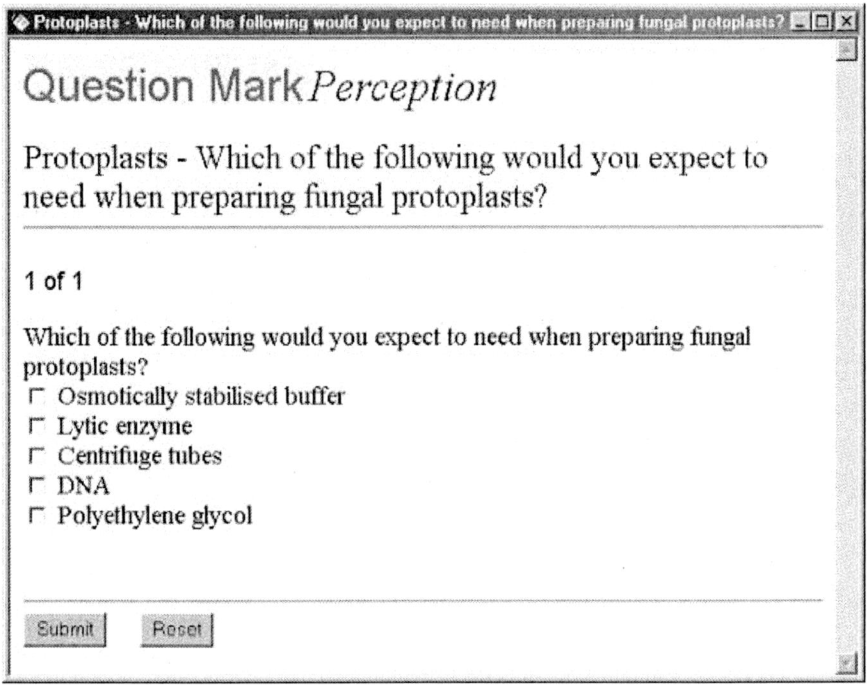

Figure 18   An example of a multiple response question prepared using Question Mark Perception

Although the Question Mark products are probably the most widely known of the commercially produced assessment software packages, there are others that are also worth investigating. For example, Interactive Assessor is a Windows-based system that allows the generation of question banks, tests and facilities for marking and analysis of results. Interactive Assessor allows students to sit a test and then locks the results of their test in a file that is accessible to the tutor, who can then use the reporter function with the software to generate, for example, marks lists.

http://www.eql.co.uk/assessor.htm

At the University of Utah a system for administering, setting and managing assessments has been developed. Web Tester allows tutors to set a variety of assessment types, including both short answer tests and essay-type questions. Although at the present time the system

http://webtester.weber.edu/default.html

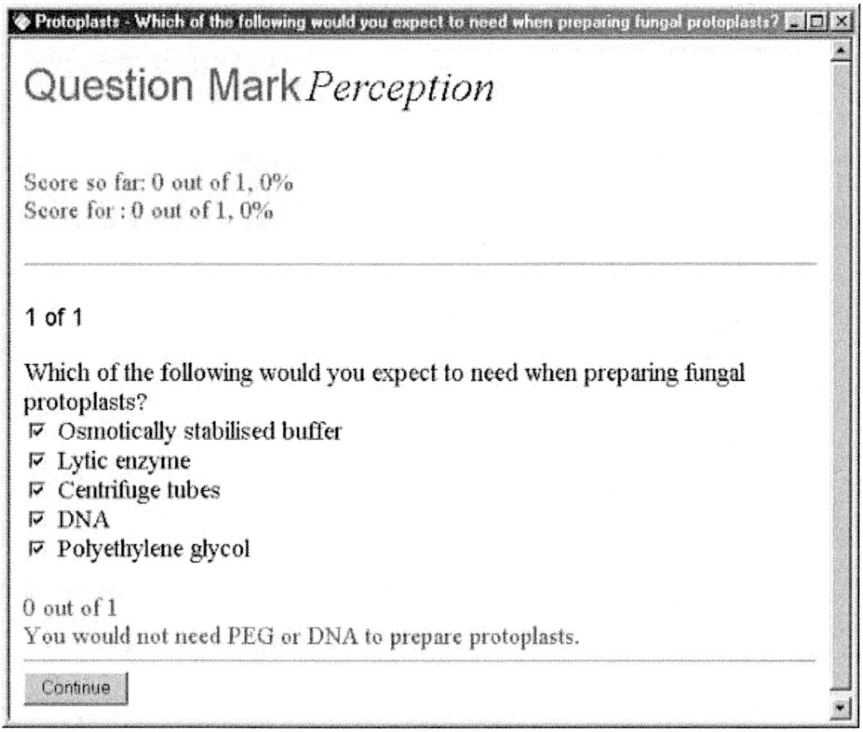

Figure 19   An example of feedback obtained by a student after clicking on the submit button shown in Figure 18

cannot mark the essay answers, it does manage to streamline many aspects of assessment management. For example, once a tutor has placed an assessment on to the Web Tester system, this can be programmed to allow access to that assessment only at a prescribed time by a predetermined set of students. Once students have logged on and completed the assessment, the system marks the answers and returns a report on each student to the tutor.

Whilst such systems can be used to provide a mark, it is of course necessary to be careful if these marks are to be used as part of the assessment towards the award that a student has registered for. With on-line assessment, especially with students based at a distance, there is always the potential for impersonation. Some care therefore needs to be taken to ensure that the individual providing the answers is who they say they are. It is *Brooks (1997)* interesting to note that David W. Brooks in his book *Web-Teaching*, asserts that taking exams over the www is possible, citing the development of image identification software as a way forward in countering the problem of impersonation.

Although it will become easier to authenticate on-line testing, it is worth pointing out that too much can be made of the potential for students to cheat using web technology. For a start it is important to remember that the potential for cheating exists with every traditional form of assessment, as much as it does for technology-based assessment. In addition, it must be remembered that cheating is a minority activity. If it is a major concern, however, there are existing 'low technology' options to consider, that normally involve some form of supervision at the location where the test is taken. As a last word on the issue of high technology cheating, it might make general sense to ensure that scarce resources are used to address issues that affect the majority (such as staff training in the use of technology) rather than invested in developing systems designed to catch the occasional cheat.

Whilst tests comprising questions of the type shown in Figure 19 already have their place in assessment regimes, there is the risk that these will be used more frequently as more staff are able to access the software that allows on-line marking and feedback elements. The use of such tests should be carefully monitored. This is important since there is no doubt that some students will find on-line testing impersonal and will therefore be uneasy with it. The risk is that a tutor makes the questions relatively easy, in an attempt to win students over and boost their confidence. This should be avoided: students can be seriously misled if tests are not sufficiently demanding and there is also the risk that they will encourage rote learning. Like any assessment method, on-line testing should be used in conjunction with other forms of assessment. In addition, questions need to be of the type that require thought and analysis in addition to a grasp of the facts.

Tracking student progress As student numbers have increased it has become difficult for staff to diagnose individual learning problems as they arise during a course. Equally, it is not necessarily easy, despite the widespread use of student feedback questionnaires, to know which parts of a course students find difficult or which they most enjoy. There is an urgent need to explore ways that can be used to identify rapidly which students are having problems through a course, in order to have the time for some remedial activity. Naturally, with a predominantly on-line course there is an additional need for some form of monitoring of student activity. This is related to the fact that, even with basic on-line material, there is the possibility that a tutor will rarely see all students taking a course.

It is possible with most specialist computer-based learning systems to keep a careful track of student activity. For example, with the learning environment software WEBCT (see Chapter 4) the student tracking function records both the first and last time that a student has accessed the course. The software is also capable of providing information on how students use the on-line material in relation to specific web pages. With such a tracking facility it is possible to determine which pages students spend more time on, which pages are visited most often and which are habitually avoided. Similarly, the record keeping function of Question Mark Perception allows a tutor to keep track of whether students are attempting formative tests and how successful they are at them.

Summary

- Assessment constitutes a major burden to the majority of academic staff.
- Computers can contribute in a number of ways in the assessment process.
- There are several software packages that enable anyone to compose on-line tests.
- On-line tests offer several advantages over conventional mechanisms for assessment, including instant marking and feedback.
- It is not the case that short answer tests can only be used to test factual recall.
- Assessment and learning software often have built-in tracking and record keeping functions.

Nine

Developing the use of web technology – an institutional approach

Two years ago the University of Westminster initiated a programme designed to enable the majority of its staff to make use of web technology. To achieve this the institution established an intranet and an associated staff development programme. This chapter describes the progress made, highlighting the successes, the problems encountered and the failings of the approach taken.

So far the chapters in this book have been written primarily to provide guidance to academic staff who are not computer experts. This chapter may, at first sight, appear to be of greater interest to those who manage the ICT function within institutions and those charged with staff development responsibilities. Evidence derived from the provision of training and guidance to many staff on the use of ICT in teaching and learning, however, supports the view that an institution's outlook on these issues is significant to both individual and cognate groups of academic staff. The reasons for this are manifold and include:

- the desire for guidance on what is essentially a new aspect to the work of staff in further and higher education
- a desire among staff to develop something that is approved by those who lead and manage the institution
- a need to believe that an approach which may reduce traditional contact time with students will not be seen as an opportunity to reduce staffing
- the desire to belong to something that goes beyond the boundaries of an individual area of work and that therefore has a better chance to attract support.

The approach at the University of Westminster 1997–1999 In 1997 the university published a new strategic plan under the leadership of a new Vice-Chancellor. The document included some bold statements about the future development of ICT across the institution, both for the management of information and to support the teaching function.

At that time, in common with other institutions, only a few staff used computers extensively in their delivery or support of teaching and learning. Those who did were mainly individuals who had been involved in government-sponsored material development schemes (such as TLTP and the CTI), a few staff who had opportunistically found computer-based material developed elsewhere that they could use, and staff in computer science. Several in computer science had been providing their students with web-based support material (lecture notes, course outlines) and some were developing their own computer-based on-line learning environment packages, as well as using automatic assessment of multiple choice tests. This left, at a conservative estimate, around 95% of staff in the institution either not using computers in teaching and learning at all, or mainly just using e-mail to maintain contact with their students.

Just after the new strategic plan was published, the Vice-Chancellor decided to devote the entire University Development Fund to teaching and learning issues for the next three years, including the development of computer-based teaching and learning approaches. A major aim was to find a way to rapidly engage a significant number of staff in using the university computer network. Externally, most computer-based material development was beginning to shift away from stand-alone CD-ROMs to material that could be integrated with the World Wide Web (www). In addition, the www offered many simple opportunities for staff to begin to provide information to students via computers and to interact remotely with users. A decision was subsequently taken to develop an institution-wide intranet service for staff and students.

The intranet project Those responsible for the proposed development reasoned that, if an identifiable and user-friendly intranet could be established and made widely available to staff, a flood of information would be published reasonably quickly. There was little doubt that many staff wanted to use the latest technology but were prevented from doing so by the perception that to write and publish a web page required a high degree of technical skill and knowledge. A major challenge for the intranet project was to demystify the whole process, and allow anyone who was prepared to try using web technology to get started. Of course, to achieve this did not necessarily require the development of an intranet; most staff are more comfortable with providing information to students via a private network. But it was reasoned that establishing an intranet would be a good way to develop a community spirit about the use of web technology.

As in many other institutions there had already been some development of the use of the www to provide information and some teaching and learning materials to students. Unless you were a computer scientist (with your own intranet), or you knew someone in the computer centre, however, you had little choice but to publish material in an unprotected fashion on the www. Although individual departments usually had at least one person designated as a www editor, these individuals had little, if any, time to help others begin to use the medium and were primarily concerned with ensuring that their department's course information on the www was up to date.

On the Microsoft Internet web site it is possible to *http://* download a document called 'The Microsoft 60 Minute *www.microsoft.com/* Intranet Kit'. Sixty minutes is optimistic but as anyone who has the technical skills will know, establishing an intranet need not take long. Provided that there is a will to have an intranet and a subsequent desire to use it, there will be someone in the central computing department who can do it. It may be necessary to purchase a computer to act as the host for the intranet (the server), but even this will not always be essential as an intranet can be established as a discrete part of an existing server.

What is useful about the Microsoft Intranet solution is the availability of a server operating system (Windows NT Server) that dovetails with Microsoft Frontpage (see Chapter 4 for more detail). There is a cautionary note here for those involved in staff development. A number of staff in universities dislike the notion of widespread adoption of software developed by corporate giants. The intranet project at the University of Westminster has shown that every web beginner who has encountered this software has ended up appreciating it. So many have commented on the ease with which this software/operating system combination has allowed them to join the techno-world of web publishing and communication. There are other software/hardware/operating system combinations that would work, but the Microsoft option was chosen mainly on the basis of relatively low cost and ease of use. Perhaps most importantly, Microsoft Frontpage places considerable control in the hands of the individual academic over his or her own material.

Launching the intranet Establishing the intranet was achieved relatively quickly. Preparing material for publication for an official launch, however, took a little longer than the 60-minute period proposed by Microsoft. It was felt sensible to begin the usable life of the intranet with material that would, in principle, be useful to all staff and students. Work therefore began on converting existing tomes, such as the academic regulations as well as smaller documents produced by the Academic Registrar's department, such as the Student Representative 's Handbook. Other central departments also provided material to go on the intranet and the project employed the services of a recent graduate full-time for about two months to convert the material into hyperlinked pages. This was no easy feat at the time, mainly because parts of certain documents existed in different formats. For example, some of the academic regulations had been produced in Word, some in an old version of Wordperfect, whilst other documents had originally been produced in a Macintosh word processing package. A great deal of time was subsequently spent on dealing with the formatting changes that arose during conversion of all of these documents to HTML.

That notwithstanding, the intranet was opened officially by the Vice-Chancellor of the university in June 1998. A reception was held to celebrate the event and a report appeared on the front page of the staff newsletter. The involvement of the Vice-Chancellor in the project was considered vital in the efforts to convince staff of the value of the intranet to them, not only for the storage and retrieval of information, but also for the support and provision of teaching and learning. There is ample anecdotal evidence to show that the seriousness with which the development was taken by a large proportion of staff was related to the perceived support of the senior figure within the institution.

At the launch of the intranet seven central departments, including the vice-chancellor's office, had web sites. Since then, the number of central departments with web sites has grown and the intranet is used increasingly both to conduct business and to raise awareness of events (see Figure 20).

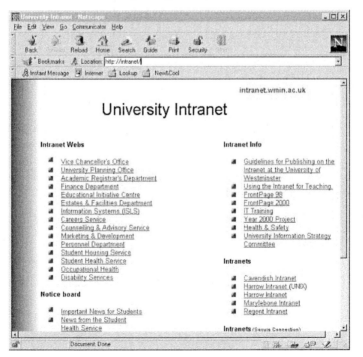

Figure 20 The university intranet system

Staff development and training At the same time as material from central departments was being converted into web pages, training for all groups of staff was initiated. In the first instance this involved one-to-one or at most one-to-two training for staff in central departments who were to be subsequently responsible for maintaining departmental intranet sites. The training was focused around the use of Microsoft Frontpage and the interaction between that software and the intranet server. By July 1998 a half-day course on using the www in teaching was being offered to academic staff. The course provided hands-on experience of the preparation and publication of pages with text and images as well as the preparation of interactive forms that could be used to elicit information from users of the material. Over the next two or three months the course ran six times with small groups of no more than six staff. Participants included the Vice-Chancellor.

Although the half-day course referred to above was received well by participants, its major value was to raise the awareness of the intranet and indeed the whole issue of using ICT in teaching. Only a small proportion of staff (around 10%) who attended the course went on, in the next six to twelve months, to establish a teaching site on the intranet. Because of this, the overall approach to staff development was altered in an attempt to realise more post-training activity from staff.

One-to-one training sessions, although obviously more costly in staff time, had previously been shown to be of great value. Individual attention seemed to stimulate more staff subsequently to publish information related to their teaching on the intranet. It was noticeable that staff were encouraged when they could arrive with some material, perhaps a Powerpoint presentation, and leave having converted it into a web-based presentation that could be accessed by all the students taking their course. Another approach involved holding open meetings with cognate groups of staff. These sessions typically included demonstrations of the use of web-based materials in teaching and learning. A significant proportion of those who attended such meetings sought further one-to-one training (or occasionally small group sessions) and went on to establish web sites. The success of this approach was evident across several disparate academic disciplines, suggesting that it was worthwhile trying the approach for almost all groups of academic staff.

From read only to useful At first, most of the information placed on the intranet was text-based and 'read only'. Right from the beginning there were efforts to break up large documents into manageable chunks of information. One immediate advantage observed by many beginners on the course referred to above was the way in which information on different departmental sites could be referenced and cross-linked. This is one of the major features of the www that applies equally to information posted on an intranet.

It was also immediately clear that a number of administrative staff wanted to use the intranet to provide users with forms that were normally distributed in hard copy. A number of central departments have now posted forms on to the intranet so that users can either download them in a useful format (e.g. MSWord) or fill them in and submit them on-line. Also academic staff were concerned if all that they were making available was 'read only' information. When staff realised that there were a lot of simple things that they could do to support a traditional course, they tended to think of ways to use on-line material more creatively. In addition, surveys have shown how appreciative students generally are about the provision of information in electronic form.

Some successes and some problems Two years after the start of the development of the intranet, the general view at Westminster is that considerable progress has been made but much remains to be done. Of course, such a development can only go a certain distance without appropriate review and changes to the whole gamut of institutional policies and strategies. For example, where open/independent learning is a major goal, the development of an intranet can certainly help. Progress towards the goal will never be total, however, if an institution finds it necessary to persist with a system that measures teaching activity in terms of contact hours.

A number of factors have been important in making the rapid progress evident so far. These include the constant involvement of senior staff and the mobilisation of internal communication mechanisms to raise awareness of the intranet. Communication of the development to all staff has included the publication of a protocol for use of the intranet and an official launch that was reported in the staff newsletter. The involvement of senior staff has helped ensure that the development has remained closely focused to institutional plans and related to available internal funding.

Staff development has also helped to publicise the existence of the intranet. It has proved particularly useful to focus training sessions, at least in the first instance, on the web and its potential, whilst highlighting strongly the ease with which novices can write and publish web pages. It is also important, right from the beginning, to ensure that staff are aware that the www can be used to support a traditional course rather than to replace it with an electronic distance learning version. It has also been noticeable that staff who have attended training are especially appreciative of any on-line support that they can subsequently access.

The institution-wide approach has not unexpectedly encountered a number of difficulties. As might have been predicted, it quickly became clear that the major obstacle to the development of on-line learning approaches was one of time. Time needs to be found to create some material in the first place. This is never easy when, as is currently the case in most institutions, the majority of staff rely heavily on a mix of lectures and hard-copy handouts. Subsequently, more time has to be invested in finding the best way to use on-line material and also on updating and improving it. The time factor was, however, compounded by the majority conception that staff could not easily acquire the skills or knowledge to utilise the available technology.

In some institutions academic staff can pass material in hard copy or electronic form to support staff who will make the material available on the network. With this approach, however, there is the risk that an academic will not be able to exploit all the creative opportunities that electronic distribution and use of materials allow. It is better for an individual to be able to prepare and work through material than rely on a third party. Material produced by a third party is difficult to use because it takes a lot of time to become sufficiently familiar with. This is so even for the simple conversion of lecture notes into web pages.

In short, the best time (which invariably belongs to the originator of the teaching material) cannot easily be bought. It is therefore essential to find a balance between doing something for someone (e.g. making some lecture notes available on the web) and developing their capability to do the same. The right circumstances and choice of software/hardware combination will help to instil confidence in beginners so that they feel eager to go beyond what they have learned in a staff development session. A critical factor in inspiring beginners is to make everything appear so easy that even they (as they will undoubtedly see it) can do it. This approach is not without risk, of course, as subsequent minor failures can become amplified by the notion of how easy it should all be. In this respect it is important to help beginners gain a sense of perspective in relation to software and hardware hiccups. Part of this involves making them aware of the role of central computing services in making everything look so simple. In addition, it is important to instil a sense of reality in their view of the fallibility of central computing services.

An effective human interface between central computing services and users has been most critical in the success of the intranet project. It is not always the case, however, that co-operation between central computing services and academic staff will automatically take place. In general, central computing services doubtless have many capable staff and sensible ideas. A significant factor in the success or otherwise of ICT-related initiatives in an institution is the degree to which it is possible to bridge the gap between the centre and the users. Whilst there is always a problem in communicating a new system to users, it helps if the system is one that the user wants and finds useful. Effective brokering between the centre and users is vital, not only to facilitate the introduction of any new system but to ensure that advances are not divorced from the overall strategies of the institution. Having said that, it is important that central computing services take a lead in the development of new systems, striking a balance between the desire to consult users and the need to ensure cost-effectiveness and facilitate timely advances in the use of technology to support teaching and learning. In this respect, at the University of Westminster the impact of one member of staff within central computing services on the overall success of the project cannot be overstated.

Choosing to make standard an operating system/ software combination, as carried out at Westminster, works best in circumstances where an institution has been able to standardise on hardware and software previously. Although many institutions are utilising mainly Microsoft products and PCs, there will always be a proportion of staff who use a different operating platform such as Macintosh or UNIX. This may be because they need to use a different platform (e.g. art and design invariably use the Macintosh platform) or because they simply choose to work outside the standard hardware specification. The best solution to the problem of user diversity is to choose for the majority, whilst trying to provide some option for the minority. An initial perception at Westminster amongst staff was that everyone had to have Microsoft Frontpage on their desktop computer for the institutional approach to work. This enabling problem was difficult to deal with at first. Clearly it is not necessary, however, for all staff to have the software on their own PC, especially when they only rarely need to update material. There have been some examples of departments at Westminster that have worked hard to expand the use of on-line learning support for their students via the intranet. In some cases they chose not to wait until each member of staff had their own copy of the required software. Instead, they found alternative working arrangements, such as the designation of one or two high specification PCs within the department as authoring and publishing channels to the intranet.

Involving students All available evidence suggests that students value the provision of teaching and learning material that supports their studies. This is perhaps not too surprising. Equally unsurprising is the fact that students of today get worried when on-line material is used to replace some of the more traditional lecturing/handout mix. If there is a major failing in the intranet project at Westminster to date, it is the failure to involve students effectively in the intranet development, right from its inception.

There is clearly little point in encouraging and enabling staff to produce electronic material for network distribution if students are not fully aware of the reasoning that lies behind making the material available in the first place. When an institution is making incremental changes to its course delivery methods, students will inevitably receive mixed messages. Whilst some modules utilise on-line materials, many will continue with a more traditional approach. In these circumstances it is essential to make students understand that there is a variety of teaching and learning approaches that they will encounter and that each one has merits if used appropriately. Some recent changes at Westminster ensure that students are clear about the teaching and learning approach used, right from the time they consider committing themselves to the institution.

Summary

- For a variety of reasons it is important that academic staff feel that the use of information and communication technology is a development that is supported by those who manage the institution.
- The involvement of senior staff, and especially the head of the institution, can have a significant impact on staff attitudes.
- Provision of courses alone is not sufficient to ensure effective take up of ICT-related opportunities.
- One-to-one training sessions and outcome-oriented workshops are the most effective ways of ensuring increased use of ICT by staff.
- The success of an institution-wide approach on the use of ICT is heavily dependent on the ability to bring together several separate constituencies.
- It is better for individual academic staff to learn how to prepare their own on-line learning materials rather than to use a third party.
- Complete progress towards the goal of open/ independent learning, including the exploitation of ICT, is dependent on appropriate changes to almost all institutional strategies.

The future use of ICT

This chapter begins by summarising current developments in teaching and learning, the role that students play and a vision for the future that provides increased opportunities for independent learning. The future use of ICT in teaching and learning, in relation to advances in technology, is considered. The chapter closes with a view of realistic changes in the use of technology that will apply to the majority of staff in institutions.

A vision for the future Predicting the future can be a complex task, requiring the merging of facts with some imagination and common sense. The accuracy or safety of predictions is usually related to the percentage of this mixture that stems from the imagination. In this chapter, the safe option, not to use the imagination too much, is taken. This seems reasonable as the problems that face further and higher education are real, not imaginary, and they deserve facts and possibilities to be combined with common sense. Any future look at the use of ICT in learning requires first a clearly defined vision of the future of learning itself.

There is little doubt that a significant number of students experience learning from the platform of *'sage on the stage'*, where a lecturer lectures and students may passively learn. The decline in frequency of small group tutorials over the past few years has almost certainly increased the preponderance of passive learning. Increasingly, new students find that college or university life is mostly about collecting a lot of paper at prearranged times and completing preset course work by a particular date, before memorising what is on the pieces of paper in order to pass the *'all important'* written examinations.

Lecturers understandably promulgate this situation by providing copious quantities of hard-copy material on prearranged dates. After all, what else can a lecturer do with a class of 50, 100 or more? How many individuals would be brave enough to go into a room full of people who are expecting one sort of event and, instead, deliver something quite different? It is true that silence can be deafening and, indeed, extremely stressful. Not surprising then is the fact that lecturing, although it too can have its stressful moments, is the method used by many academic staff.

Lecturing provides a surer way of controlling the classroom event and covers up deficiencies that exist in the further and higher education learning environment. Whilst it is not difficult to point at external factors that have created deficiencies, these factors don't count when an academic member of staff faces his or her students. At that moment the deficiencies are his or her fault. Lecturing is one simple way to appear to make up for these. Supplementing lectures with copious hard-copy notes is another way.

The part students play

Students naturally play their part in promoting passive learning – after all, it is an easy option. The extent to which individual students play this role will relate to their own circumstances and background. A student with a clear motive to learn what they need to know, (e.g. a part-time day release student whose next promotion depends on completing the course) will be keen on the lectures and printed notes approach. Mature students who inevitably have a broader range of higher level key skills (problem solving, etc.) will also be quite comfortable with rote learning if that is what is provided. Young students, fresh from school, will be happy to go along with a simple routine, often because they will need to spend less time organising their studies and therefore have more time to explore their new found independence. There are other groups of students who inevitably express relief at the availability of perceived knowledge and understanding in the form of notes and handouts. These include those who need to work in order to pay for study and those with significant external commitments, such as a young family.

Given the above, which students are left with the drive to actively seek discussion of key issues, key facts and the development of higher level skills? The answer, in higher education at least, is not many. Certainly, extremely intelligent students will probably get quite bored with a passive approach and will seek ways to challenge themselves. There may possibly be a few students who have realised that listening to lectures and taking handouts is not how it will be at work, when they will need to rely on themselves. Some students realise that employers are more likely to pay a premium for independent capabilities that may be manifested in a variety of ways, from having the confidence to speak up when no one else will to knowing a good process to follow when confronted by an unfamiliar problem.

An exciting vision of the future of learning demands that both staff and students will want to explore and exploit as many opportunities for independent active learning as they respectively can. A huge cultural shift in the perceived methods of learning is required by both camps (staff and student) in order to be sure that the future use of ICT in teaching and learning makes an effective impact. Whilst many staff need to move from being the *'sage on the stage'* to a *'guide on the side'*, students need assistance in understanding clearly their roles and responsibilities within the learning process.

The future use of ICT in learning and teaching

ICT currently has a high profile and a positive future in further and higher education, offering the potential to perform a number of activities more effectively. Changes will be made to course delivery that can affect the majority of academic staff. Will this be in a positive way?

There are several ways to begin answering this question. Initially, it is unlikely that the first 10 years of this millennium will see a wholesale shift from face-to-face based education to some kind of pseudo-distance mode, where present day traditional students spend the bulk of their time learning from a remote location and hardly ever see or speak with a tutor. This clear statement is made not because it will be impossible to achieve pseudo-distance teaching technologically, but because students won't want it. Most people do like to talk face-to-face with others and even those who don't periodically need to, in order to solve a problem or to understand a concept completely. Having said that, there are probably plenty of traditional students who would welcome the flexibility of not having to attend for classes at the traditional place of study as often as they currently do. Not having to attend for classes, however, is not the same as not having or wanting to attend the normal place of study. It is worth remembering that many students come to college or university to get away from home and develop new friendships and ways of interacting with others. The social value of modern universities and colleges in the development of people will not readily be replaced by any current or soon-to-be realised form of information technology.

Advances in technology Everyone realises how quickly technology changes and progresses. The last century began with most people in awe of the light bulb and ended with many people complaining at how long their e-mail takes to download. It does seem that the human race is currently heading for a 'chips with everything' world, where things, as well as people, will be able to think. By the end of the decade we will certainly see our friends as we contact them over long distances and our daily frustration might be rebooting the kitchen as much as it is currently re-booting our PCs. Further into the future, education might even become a concept of the past, as individuals download the brain of their choice and use it for however long they wish before they choose another. Whilst this might sound a little unreal, any reader may

Volume 10, (3), October 1999 wish to glance at an article in *Scientific American Presents* that describes the prospects of downloading brains in the twenty-first century.

In some ways, predictions of what will be happening 100 years from now have a right to appear silly, especially since the individual doing the predicting won't be around to be embarrassed when it turns out to be different. The point is that it is alright to be slightly outrageous, and perhaps not to worry too much about the consequences, when predicting what the long-term future might be. It is definitely not alright, however, to present advanced computer technologies as the white knight of learning, when the majority of teachers are still getting to grips with e-mail and are prone to alarm at the thought of being replaced by a computer.

There are also deeper considerations and concerns that require some urgent attention. Most academics decry the notion of 'fact shovelling' and yet much of the appeal of modern information technology lies in the capability to store and retrieve huge quantities of information in databases or deliver live lectures to a geographically dispersed audience. The danger of using this method of education is that it will lead to a virtual *'sage on the stage'* scenario.

A major difference between a live and virtual *'sage on the stage'* is, of course, that 'live' opportunities to individualise a topic in the latter are lost. Increasingly in this situation an opportunity is likely to become standardised and possibly therefore subject to influences that may impede freedom of thought. The current trend for corporate universities is compounding the standardisation risk and could conceivably, if left unchecked, further erode the 'citizenship' goals that once were a cornerstone of post-compulsory education.

The recent announcement by the American billionaire Michael Saylor of a free on-line university for all should serve to make the alarm bells ring that much louder. His vision of *'the world's great minds delivering lectures in streaming video over the Internet for anyone to watch and hear'* does nothing to suggest great diversity in the education that his university will offer. Nor does it, by virtue of the emphasis on lectures, imply a great belief in anything other than fact shovelling.

It is technologically possible to deliver a course in such a way that students can, in principle, never physically meet with a lecturer or tutor. Using video-conferencing and virtual reality it is possible to provide an exciting part simulated, part real (but from a distance) course. Because of the cost of such technology, however, including that incurred in the preparation of appropriate material, the majority of educational providers are excluded from making widespread use of it. There is also the problem that the recipients of such educational delivery need to have appropriate technology, in the form of hardware, software and a data link, at their location. At the present time these demands mean that the majority of students are not able to take part in an interactive video-conference, even if a college or university has the capability to mount one. It is likely that technology systems enabling interactive video-conferencing to multiple locations will become more widely usable in the near future. As already stated

http://www.ucaid.edu/

in Chapter 7, however, the cost of the increase in bandwidth required will be beyond most students for some time, potentially leaving the majority stuck with a fact-shovelling version of on-line learning.

The majority future How will the majority of staff progress with the use of ICT in teaching and learning? At the moment there is much activity across the sector that is leading to the creation of web sites by academic staff. Typically, these web sites start by making available lecture notes, handouts and various other bits of information that are normally provided to students in hard-copy. In some cases, but not all, students no longer receive hard copy material from the lecturer. They may be given summary hard-copy versions or they can be provided with the materials on a floppy disk or a CD-ROM so that they can open the files on their own home PC. Many staff are happy to do this because the conversion of existing material to electronic form can be fairly easily achieved and the time required is manageable. They can also see the potential benefits to themselves, as well as their students. Students tend to appreciate the provision of on-line support material but can be uncomfortable if this provision changes existing delivery significantly. What this illustrates, is that what actually happens in the future will reflect whether or not academic staff, and students, are able to see the potential benefits of predicted changes. Similarly, administrative staff are starting to increasing their use of ICT as they begin to see the many advantages that can be gained from its prudent use.

Table 22 attempts to list the probable developments that the majority of staff and students will participate in over the next 10 years.

Table 22   Likely future stages in the development of the use of ICT

Short term **(1–2 years)**	Availability of on-line support material will increase markedly. The use of on-line assessment, at least in the form of automatically marked MCQs, will become more commonplace. Electronic communication (e-mail) with students will become more widespread, effective and probably web-based. Increasing amounts of induction and enrolment information will become available on-line. It will become increasingly common for some students to be able to apply for courses on-line.
Medium term **(2–5 years)**	There will be an increased availability and take-up by academic staff of off-the-shelf learning material to support courses. The use of web-based video archives of lectures and tutorials, to support text- and image-based material, will increase. The effective use of on-line web-based discussion groups will increase. It will become more common for some course work to be submitted electronically. E-commerce will begin to have an impact on the way in which students pay their fees. Requirements for paper records will decline.
Long term **(5–10 years)**	Video-conferencing into the home or work place of students will be more common, allowing live interactive sessions with a geographically distributed audience. An increasing number of laboratory or studio-based sessions will be open to replacement by simulation. Face-to-face interactions between students and administrative staff will occur rarely.

For those hopelessly in awe of the latest technology the list in Table 22 may hold little appeal and may not appear terribly ambitious. Indeed, it is possible, given the advances in technology, that some factors limiting widespread implementation of some technologies may be quickly removed. In Chapter 7 reference was made to British Telecom ADSL lines that will increase Internet connection speeds by up to 40 times. At the time of writing, the first Internet enabled mobile phones are about to come on the market in the UK; and the world is about to witness Bluetooth. Apparently named after a Viking King, Bluetooth is a radiowave-based technology that will revolutionise the concept of wireless computer systems. Unlike infra red technology, any two devices that need to communicate will not need to be pointing at each other in order to do so.

To look forward realistically, however, it is necessary to forget the technology as much as possible and instead think of the changes required involving the attitude of people towards education and each other. The list in Table 22 is realistic in relation to the need to change attitudes at the same time as making progress on the effective integration of ICT in learning and teaching.

ICT will undoubtedly play an increasing role in the lives of academic staff and students. The extent to which that will be useful to participants, however, will depend on the speed with which institutional structures and procedures, as well as attitudes of staff and students, can be opened up to the possibilities. A change is unlikely to occur as quickly as some technologists would like. Technology will have to wait whilst pedagogy, in all of its manifestations, asserts itself as the driving force behind its use. By the same token pedagogists should do all that they can to become a driving force faster than they might like, in order to be able to build a working partnership with students of this millennium.

Hopefully, by the time that talking to another person or group of people at any time, from any location to any other location, becomes as easy and cheap as making a phone call, all stakeholders in further and higher education will have already seen that information technology's major role in education is to facilitate and enhance opportunities for discussion and active learning.

Summary

- Lecturers still often give out copious notes although some are beginning to use web sites to communicate with students.
- The aim of staff and students should be for active learning to take place using whichever medium is the most appropriate.
- In the immediate future, there is likely to be a shift from face-to-face learning to distance learning.
- Video-conferencing is an exciting way of providing distance learning.
- A change is required to attitudes towards education in order for ICT to be integrated appropriately into teaching and learning.

Glossary

Attachment A file that is sent together with an e-mail message.

Application A program that serves the user, as opposed to those that control the computer (systems programs).

ASCII Acronym for American standard code for information interchange. In this coding system, letters digits and punctuation symbols are assigned numbers. Computers use the system for storage of text and data transmission.

Back-up Copy of a file that is made so that the file may be restored in case of a fault in the system or file itself. Many applications create back-up files.

Bandwidth The rate that data is transmitted. Bandwidth is measured in bits per second.

Browse To search and view data on the World Wide Web.

Bulletin board A centre for the electronic storage of messages, notices and programs dedicated to specific interest groups which may be accessed through a network via e-mail.

CBLM Commonly used abbreviation for computer-based learning material.

CBT Commonly used abbreviation for computer-based training.

CD-ROM Computer storage device that can be read optically by passing a light beam over the disk. Can hold about 550 Mb of data and is used for distributing large text and graphic files.

Chat area Part of an on-line learning environment that is used for exchange of information that may not be of an academic nature.

Compound editors Web authoring software combining a WYSIWYG user interface with the capability to introduce HTML.

Computer-assisted learning Using computers in education and training. Instructions to the exercise are displayed, the computer then asks questions about the information provided; the order of exercises is dependent on the answers given.

Computer peripherals An item of equipment attached to and controlled by the computer. Principally used for input from and output to the user, data storage and communication. For example, keyboard, printer, disk drive, modem, etc.

Computer workstation A desktop computer capable of high performance with strong graphics capabilities and good networking facilities.

CPU Abbreviation for central processing unit.

Crash Freezing the screen.

Data projector Physical device that enables signals from a PC to be projected on to a screen.

Database Data collection in a structured format. Allows manipulation of data to select and sort desired information.

Desktop applications and files These are represented by pictures (icons) on the computer screen and can be triggered by clicking the mouse.

Desktop publishing (DTP) System for small scale typesetting and page layout. Used to prepare camera-ready pages consisting of text and graphics, or for an electronic printer.

Dial-up networking facility A system that allows connection to the Internet via a telephone line.

Digital image The image is represented as a quantity by coding into numbers and storing as data.

Digital video (or versatile) (DVD) drive/disks High capacity optical disks. DVDs are double-sided, each side capable of storing in excess of 4.7 Gb.

Directory A list of file names and information that is stored by the computer and used to retrieve files.

Discussion web A web site that allows users to submit views or articles on a particular theme as well as reading and responding to use or articles posted by others.

Distribution list A list of e-mail addresses to which a message will be automatically sent.

Dot matrix printer Each character is printed by individually printing a pattern of very small dots.

Download To copy information from one computer to another via a network.

Drag and drop Physically moving files between locations using the mouse.

Educational licence Special discounted rate for software supplied for the purposes of education.

Electronic media Computer-based information.

Electronic teaching aids General term used to describe normally physical tools used to facilitate the delivery of learning material.

e-mail Electronic mail enables messages to be sent between users of a computer network using telephone wires to send signals from terminal to terminal.

Encrypt Encoding data in order to secure it. Without decoding software, this information is meaningless.

Ethernet card A protocol for local area networks that transfers data at a rate of up to 10 Mbps.

Export file File is stored in a format that can be accessed by other programs or computers. When this file is accessed by the second program or computer, it is referred to as an import file.

Field A specific item of data often part of a record. Occurs in spreadsheets and databases.

File format The structure of the data in the file.

File transfer The transmission of data between computers which are physically linked and running appropriate software.

File transfer protocol (FTP) Transmission of files over the Internet.

Filename The name given to a collection of data (file).

Firewall Software that is used to protect internal networks from the intrusions of hackers.

Floppy disk Light, flexible storage disk which is approximately 3.5 inches in diameter.

Folder A group of files which are stored under the same heading.

Font A particular style applied to a set of printable characters.

Freeware Software that can be freely used by all.

GIF format A bit-mapped, graphic file format used by Compuserve and other Bulletin boards.

Gigabyte (Gb) A unit of memory capacity which is equivalent to 1,024 Mb.

Graphical web browser A web browser that operates on a point and click basis.

Graphics card A printed circuit board that is required by the computer in order for it to display graphics.

Group work area An area within an on-line learning environment which is only usable by a specified group of students.

Hard disk drive A huge storage device in the computer. The hard disk drive is the computer's workhorse. It runs continuously all the time the computer is switched on, holding programs and data ready for use as requested.

Hardware The physical components of a computer which include electronic, electrical and mechanical constituents. This may also include the computer's power supply, its processing unit housing, circuit boards, screen, disk drives, keyboard and printer.

Helper application Helps a web browser to use files that cannot be opened/ read directly by the browser.

HiFD High density floppy disk drive.

Homepage The main page in the web site.

Hyperlink A link between documents or within a document. The link is usually highlighted in some way and can be activated by clicking on it with the mouse.

Hypertext mark-up language (HTML) The language in which web pages are written.

Icon A small picture on the computer screen representing a data file or program. Clicking on the icon with the mouse activates the function.

ICT Commonly used abbreviation for information and communication technology.

Image tag HTML tag that instructs a web browser to display an image.

Import See export.

Information superhighway A term coined by US vice president Al Gore to describe the Internet and other related large-scale computer networks.

Information technology (IT) Describes the technology involved in the processing and transmission of information.

Infra red transfer Use of infra red signals to issue commands to PCs and PC peripherals.

Ink jet printer This printer creates characters and graphics by spraying very fine jets of quick-drying ink on to paper. Provides good quality, inexpensive printing.

Institutional networks An example of these is JANET (see below).

Integrated learning systems Another term used to describe an on-line learning system that includes several features such as on-line notes, discussion areas and interactive exercises.

Interactive multimedia materials (IMM) A computer system that will respond directly to data or commands, enabling the user to specify the type of information displayed and to choose a route through the information.

Interface The point of contact between two programs or pieces of equipment. For example, the connection between a computer and peripheral device.

Internet A global, on-line computer network connecting governments, academic institutions, commerce and private users.

Internet relay chat A web-based chat system where any message that you type is immediately transmitted to all of the other people involved in the chat session.

Internet service provider (ISP) Specialist providers of dial-up Internet connections.

Intranet A secure computer network consisting of information for access by specific users. For example, a network that can only be accessed by University of Westminster staff.

Jaz drive Peripheral storage device taking 1 Gb or 2 Gb disks and transfer rates of over 5 Mbps.

Joint academic network (JANET) A centrally funded network that links almost all universities in the UK.

JPEG format Abbreviation for joint photographic experts group. A graphic file format used for storage and transmission of images.

Keyboard An input device resembling a typewriter keyboard which is used to input data and instructions to the computer.

LAN Abbreviation for local area network. This network can be restricted to a single room or building.

Laser printer The text or image to be printed is formed by the action of a laser on a light-sensitive drum and then transferred to paper by means of an electrostatic charge. These printers produce very high quality print, and black and white ones are relatively inexpensive.

LCD Abbreviation for liquid crystal display.

Learning environment packages Specialised software that allows the establishment of a multifunctional on-line environment containing learning materials and permitting interaction between students and students and tutor.

Local area network (LAN) A network of computers restricted to a room or building.

Log on The process by which a user identifies himself to a multi-user computer (usually by entering a password) before access to the system is allowed.

LS120 disk A storage device similar in size and interchangeable with a 3.5 inch floppy disk but which has a storage capacity of 120 MB.

Macintosh A range of computers produced by Apple Computers which were the first to use a graphical user interface. Macintosh computers are still widely used in the design and graphics industry.

Mail client A software package that allows a user to download e-mail messages from a mail server on to a desktop PC.

Mailbase An e-mail system hosted via the University of Newcastle that enables academics to set up a mailing list that might be used, for example, for discussion groups or for electronic meetings.

Managed learning environments Another term for learning environment packages.

Megabyte (Mb) A unit of memory which is equivalent to 1,024 Kb.

Megahertz (MHz) 1,000,000 clock signals a second (computers are often compared according to the so-called clock speed of the computer processor).

Memory device Part of the computer system which is used to store data and programs, either permanently or temporarily.

Menu driven options A list of options displayed on the computer screen from which the user may choose by pointing and clicking the mouse.

Microchip Commonly used term for the silicon chip or integrated circuit.

Microsoft Internet Explorer A web browser - a program allowing the user to search and view documents on the World Wide Web.

Modem Acronym for modulator/demodulator. A peripheral device used for transmitting data over telephone lines between computers.

Monitor Computer screen.

Motherboard A printed circuit board containing the main components of a computer such as the power, memory capacity and capability for enhancement by addition of expansion boards to the motherboard.

Mouse An input device which is a feature of graphical user interface and used to control a pointer on the computer screen.

MS-DOS Abbreviation for Microsoft disk operating system. A computer operating system developed by the Microsoft Corporation and widely used in computers with Intel X 86 family microprocessors.

Multimedia The use of text, sound and graphics to create an interactive application. For example, a database of animals that allows a user to search and retrieve text, pictures and video clips as well as hear sounds that the animals make.

Navigation aid A system of links designed to permit users to find their way around a web site.

Navigation structure A diagram which shows the way in which pages that make up a web site are interconnected via hyperlinks.

Netscape Navigator Web browser. See Microsoft Internet Explorer.

Network computers Network computers are connected together to share data and/or peripheral devices.

Network card Each computer requires a suitable network interface card in order for it to be successfully linked to a network of computers.

Network port Also referred to as the universal serial bus (USB). An interface connected at the network port enables the computer to communicate with the network.

Networking devices Computer hardware, such as a modem or an Ethernet card, that allows individual computers to be connected to the Internet.

Newsgroup A discussion group on the Internet.

Notice-board area An area within an on-line learning environment where notices are posted for students and staff.

On-line learning Learning using data transferred through connection to a network.

On-line messaging system Web-based messaging system.

Operating system (OS) A program that controls the basic operation of the computer. The operating system controls the communications from users and application software with the computer hardware.

Optical storage device Laser technology is used to record and read large volumes of digital data on to optical disks (e.g. CD-ROM).

Palm top computers Small, virtually pocket-sized computers which run Windows-driven software. Can be linked to most desktop PCs.

Password Secret combination of characters used to ensure data security.

Pentium processor A microchip produced by Intel, which is the central processing unit in most PCs. Currently, the most widely used CPUs include Pentium II and Pentium III processors.

Personal computer (PC) A term for microcomputer or more specifically to mean IBM personal computer or IBM compatible.

Plug-in A program that a web browser may use to display a file that the browser itself cannot read.

Portable computers Computers which are small and compact enough to be transported from place to place. These include laptops, palm top, notebook and sub-notebook computers.

Printer Output device connected to a computer and used to print text and graphics. Printers most commonly used are ink jet and laser printers.

Program A set of instructions that control the computer. Programs can be written in a number of programming languages which are then converted to two machine codes before they are executed by the computer.

Proxy server A server is a computer that acts as a data store for other computers on a network.

RAM Abbreviation for random access memory. A memory device in the form of a collection of microchips. The computer can both read from and write to RAM chips but their contents are lost once the computer is switched off.

Reboot To restart computer.

Reflector site A location which receives a video-conference and broadcasts the signal to multiple users at multiple locations.

Remote computer Used to communicate with a mainframe computer via a modem and telephone line.

Restricted access Protecting data by only allowing access to users with passwords.

Scanner peripheral A device used to produce a digital copy of the document for input and storage in computer. Widely used to store digital copies of images. To enable editing of text input using a scanner, suitable optical character recognition (OCR) software is required.

Scrolling The process by which data is displayed on a computer screen, automatically moving upwards and out of sight as new data is added to the bottom.

Search engine A facility that allows the user to search the Internet specifically for topics of interest. For example, Yahoo, Infoseek, Excite.

Searchable database A database that has a search facility which allows the user to search and view specific items of interest.

Server A server is a computer that acts as a data store for other computers on a network.

Shareware Software that is distributed principally to allow users to test its functionality and suitability to the user's requirements. If the user decides to use the software, they are asked to pay a small registration fee directly to the author. Shareware is not copyright-free.

Shortcut An icon that can be present on a PC desktop and that acts as a fast route to a particular location or software.

Site licence A software licence agreement that covers the use of that software package amongst computers at a particular location.

Site manager Software that allows folders and files within a web site to be visualised graphically and managed.

Software Consists of programs and procedures which enable a computer to perform a specific task. Computers cannot function without software. Distributed on medium such as floppy disks, CD-ROM, etc.

Software bundle or pack Collection of individual pieces of software.

Soundcard A printed circuit board that when added to a computer and coupled to speakers enables the computer to reproduce sound and music.

Spreadsheet A program in which the computer screen is divided into rows and columns. A user can enter values into the rows and columns on the sheet and then instruct the computer to perform a calculation. This may be as simple as the summation of the contents of a row or as complex as applying a formula to certain values. A common spreadsheet program is Excel.

Sub directory A folder within a folder.

Surfing A term applied to the time spent searching and viewing documents on the World Wide Web.

Tag A unit of HTML code.

TCP/IP An abbreviation for transport control protocol/Internet protocol. This is a set of network protocols which is widely used in UNIX and on the Internet.

Telnet Software that enables a user to access a computer from a remote location.

Template Determines the basic structure for a document and contains document settings such as fonts, page layout, special formatting and styles. Many programs allow the user to create their own templates. For example, templates for a newsletter.

Text file A file that can be opened and read by software that can read ASCII text.

Thumbnail A miniaturised image.

Universal resource location (URL) A web address of a document. The URL allows a user to locate a document on the web.

UNIX A multiuser operating system.

Upload Data is sent from a computer to a storage device or across a network.

User-friendly A term used to describe the ease of using a computer system.

Username The name allocated to a user (usually along with a password) to allow access to restricted area/data.

Video card A printed circuit board within a PC that facilitates the display of images on the computer screen. Also commonly known as the graphics card.

Video-conference Remote conferencing allowing participants to both see and hear each other in real time.

Virtual Not physically present but treated as if it was.

Virus A program that can replicate and transfer itself between computers without the user being aware, causing undesirable and destructive effects to computer data.

Virus protection software Software designed to detect viruses, alert the user and remove virus programs before they can act. Virus protection software should be updated regularly in order for it to be effective against new viruses.

Visual aids Physical devices such as slide projector or overhead projector that help to illustrate a presentation.

Web address See Universal Resource Location.

Web authoring Creating documents for publishing on the World Wide Web.

Web-based learning A form of learning that relies wholly or in part on the use of web-based resources that may be on the Internet or on an intranet.

Web browser Allows user to search and view documents on the World Wide Web. Data may not be edited but sometimes it is possible to save or download data and convert it to different file formats.

Web page A text file written in HTML that allows a web browser to display text and images and incorporate sound and video according to the HTML code.

Web site A term used to describe a collection of web documents within a single URL on the web.

Windows A graphical user interface produced by Microsoft that is standard for IBM PCs.

Windows NT A multiuser and multitasking operating system based on Windows produced by Microsoft.

Wizard A series of dialogue boxes that takes the user through an organised procedure.

Word processing Used to describe storage and retrieval of written text by a computer.

World Wide Web (www) A network of computer-based resources for publishing information which is available over the Internet.

Zip drive A peripheral storage device popular for transporting and backing up data. Uses 250 Mb or 100 Mb disks as storage medium.

References

Abercrombie, M. L. J. (1979) *Aims and Techniques of Group Teaching* Society for Research into Higher Education, Guildford

Ashcroft, K. and Foreman-Peck, L. (1998) *Managing Teaching and Learning in Further and Higher Education* The Falmer Press

Ause, W., Arpajian, S. and Ivens, K. (1997) *How to Use the World Wide Web* MacMillan Computer Publishing, USA

Austin, B. (1998) *Web Page Design in Easy Steps* Computer Step, Warwickshire, UK

Ausubel, D. P. (1968) *Educational Psychology: A Cognitive View* Holt, Rinehart and Winston, New York

Barrie, J. M. (1996) *The World Wide Web as an Instructional Tool* Science, 274, 371-372

Bates, A. (1991) *Third Generation Distance Education: The Challenge of new Technology* Research in Distance Education, 3(2) 10-15.

Bates, A. W. (1995) *Technology, Open Learning and Distance Education* Routledge, London

Beard, R. and Hartley, J. (1984) *Teaching and Learning in Higher Education* Paul Chapman, London

Beard, R. M. and Senior, I. J. (1980) *Motivating Students* Routledge and Kegan Paul, London

Behr, A. L. (1988) *Exploring the Lecture Method: An Empirical Study* Studies in Higher Education, 13(2), 154 – 163

Bell, M. (1993) *IT in Learning* The Computer Bulletin, April

Berge, L. Z. (1995) *Computer Mediated Communications and the On-Line Classroom* Vol II. Higher Education, Hampton Press, Cresskill NJ

Berners-Leigh, T. (1999) *Weaving the Web* Harper, San Francisco

Biggs, J. B. and Moore, P. J. (1993) *The Process of Learning* Prentice-Hall, Sydney

Bligh, D. A. (1971) *What's the Use of Lectures?* Penguin, Harmondsworth

Bliss, J. and Ogborn J. (Eds) (1977) *Students' Reactions to Undergraduate Science* Nuffield Foundation Higher Education Learning Project, Physics Heinemann, London

Boud, D. and Felleti, G. (Eds) (1991) *The Challenge of Problem Based Learning* Kogan Page, London

Brooks, D. W. (1997) *Web-Teaching: A Guide to Designing Interactive Teaching for the World Wide Web* Plenum Press, New York

Brown, G. and Atkins, M. (1988) *Effective Teaching in Higher Education* Methuen, London

Brown, G. A. and Bakhtar, M. (Eds) (1983) *Styles of Lecturing* ASTD Publications, University of Loughborough

Brown, G., Bull, J. and Race, P. (Eds) (1999) *Computer Assisted Assessment of Students* Kogan Page, London

Brown, S., Race, P. and Smith, B. (1996) *500 Tips on Assessment* Kogan Page, London

Brown, S. and Smith, B. (Eds) (1996) *Resource Based Learning* Kogan Page, London

Cassanova, J. and Cassanova, S. L. (1991) *Computers in the Classroom – What Works and What Doesn't* Computers in Chemical Education Newsletter (Spring), 5 – 9

Chacon, F. (1992) *A Taxonomy of Computer Media in Distance Education* Journal of Open and Distance Learning, 7(1) 12-27

Chalmers, D. and Fuller, R. (1996) *Teaching and Learning at University* Kogan Page, London

Entwistle, N. J. and Ramsden, P. (1983) *Understanding Student Learning* Croom Helm, London

Evans, T. (1998) *HTML 4, 10 Minute Guide* Que, Indianapolis USA

Forsyth, I. (1998) *Teaching and Learning Materials and the Internet* Kogan Page, London

Gibbs, G. (1995) *Research into Student Learning* in: B. Smith and S. Brown (Eds) *Research Teaching and Learning* pp 19 – 29, Kogan Page

Gibbs, G., Habeshaw, S. and Habeshaw, T. (1986) *53 Interesting ways to Assess your Students* Technical and Educational Services, Bristol

Gibbs, G., Habeshaw, S. and Habeshaw, T. (1992) *53 Interesting Things to do in your Lectures* Technical and Educational Services, Bristol

Gibbs, G. and Habeshaw, T. (1998) *Preparing to Teach: An Introduction to Effective Teaching in Higher Education* Cromwell Press, UK

Gibbs, G. and Jenkins, A. (Eds) (1992) *Teaching Large Classes in Higher Education: How to maintain quality with reduced resources* Kogan Page, London

Goodlad, S. (1989) *Peer Tutoring* Kogan Page, London

Hartley, J. (1983) *Notetaking Research: Resetting the Scoreboard* Bulletin of the British Psychological Society, 36, pp 13 – 14

Heinich, R., Molenda, M., Russell, J. D. and Smaldino, S. E. (1996) *Instructional Media and Technologies for Learning* Prentice-Hall, Englewood Cliffs

Heywood, J. (1989) *Assessment in Higher Education* John Wiley and Sons Ltd, Chichester

Hilgard, E. R. and Bower, G. (1975) *Theories of Learning* Prentice Hall, Eaglewood Cliffs, NJ

Hiltz, S. R. (1994) *The Virtual Classroom: Learning Without Limits via Computer Networks* Ablex Publishing Corp., Norwood New Jersey

Hodgson, V. (1984) *Learning from Lectures* in: F. Marton, D. J. Hounsell and N. J. Entwistle (Eds), *The Experience of Learning* Scottish Academic Press, Edinburgh

Hofstetter, F. (1995) *Multimedia Literacy* McGraw-Hill, London

Honey, P. and Mumford A. (1986) *Using Your Learning Styles* Ardingley House (second edition)

Hudson, R., Maslin-Protheroe, S. and Oates, L. (1997) *Flexible Learning in Action. Case Studies in Higher Education* Kogan Page, London

Hundt, R. (1999) *The Telecom Act, the Internet and Higher Education* Educom Review, 34 (6) 14-19

Hurley, J. (2000) *Supporting On-Line Learning* Learning Partners

Jaques, D. (1991) *Learning in Groups* Kogan Page, London

Kent, P. (1998) *The Complete Idiots Guide to the Internet* Alpha Books, Que

Kurzweil, R. (1999) *The Coming Merging of Mind and Machine* Scientific American Presents, 10, (3), pp 56 – 62

Laurillard, D. M. (1993) *Rethinking University Teaching: A Framework for the Effective use of Educational Technology* Routledge, London

Lisewki , B. and Settle, C. (1996) S. Brown and B. Smith (Eds) (1996) *Integrating Multimedia Resource-Based Learning into the Curriculum* pp 109 – 119, Kogan Page, London

McCleish, J. (1976) *The Lecture Method* in: M. L. Gage (Ed), *Teaching Methods* National Society for the Study of Education 75th Yearbook, Chicago

McConnell, D. (1995) *Implementing Computer Supported Co-operative Learning* Kogan Page, London

McCormack, C. and Jones, D. (1998) *Building a Web Based Education System* John Wiley and Sons Ltd, Chichester

Maier, P., Barnett, L., Warren, A. and Brunner D. (1998) *Using Technology in Teaching and Learning* Kogan Page, London

Marton, F. and Saljo, R. (1984) *Approaches to Learning* in: F. Marton, D. J. Hounsell and N. J. Entwistle (Eds) *The Experience of Learning* Scottish Academic Press, Edinburgh

Morgan, C. and O'Reilly, M. (1999) *Assessing Open and Distance Learners* Kogan Page, London

Muzio, J. (1989) *E-mail and Electronic Transfer of Data Files for a Distance Education Course*, in *Mindweave: Communication, Computers and Distance Education* Pergamon, Oxford

Pescovitz, D. (1999) *Getting Real in Cyberspace* Scientific American Presents, 10 (3), 48 – 51

Phillips, R. (1997) *The Developer's Handbook to Interactive Multimedia: A Practical Guide for Educational Applications* Kogan Page, London

Polonsky, W. B. and Lehto, A. (1999) *Official Microsoft Frontpage 2000 Book* Microsoft Press, Washington

Race, P. and McDowell, S. (1996) *500 Computing Tips for Teachers and Lecturers* Kogan Page, London

Raucci, R. (1995) *Mosaic for Windows* Springer-Verlag, New York

Reeves, T. C. (1992) *Evaluating Interactive Multimedia* Educational Technology, May, 47 – 52

Romer, R. and Swanson, M. (1999) *Microsoft Office 2000 Professional at a Glance* Microsoft Press, Washington

Rowntree, D. (1992) *Exploring Open and Distance Learning* Kogan Page, London

Rust, C. and Wisdom, J. (1996) in: S. Brown and B. Smith (Eds) (1996) *Helping Individual Staff to Develop Resource-Based Learning* pp 38 – 48, Kogan Page, London

Sangster, A. (1995) *World Wide Web – What Can It Do for Education?* Active Learning, 2, 17 – 18

Saunders, G., Rumpus, A. and McShane, D. (1999) *An Evaluation of the Use of the World Wide Web for Module Delivery* in: P. Marquet, S. Mathey, A. Jaillet and E. Nissen (Eds), *Internet Based Teaching and Learning* (IN-TELE) 98, pp545 – 550 Peter Lang, GmbH.

Smith, C. (1997) *Teaching by E-mail* in: R. Hudson, S. Maslin-Protheroe and L. Oates (Eds) *Flexible Learning in Action. Case Studies in Higher Education* pp 34 – 38 Kogan Page, London

Smith, R. M. (1983) *Learning How to Learn: Applied Theory for Adults* Open University Press, Buckingham

Sosabowski, M.H., Herson, K. and Lloyd, A.W. (1998) *Identifying and Overcoming Staff Resistance to Computer Based Learning and Teaching Methods: Shedding Milestones to Achieve Milestones* Active Learning, 9, 26 – 30

Talbott, S. (1999) *Who's Killing Higher Education?* Educom Review, 34(2), 26 – 33

Trigwell, K. and Prosser, M. (1991) *Relating Approaches to Study and Quality of Learning Outcomes at the Course Level,* British Journal of Educational Psychology, 61, 265 – 275

Warren, A., Brunner, D., Maier, P. and Barnett, L. (1998) *Technology in Teaching and Learning: An Introductory Guide,* Kogan Page, London

Watkins, D. A. and Hattie, J. (1985) *A Longitudinal Study of the Approach to Learning of Australian Tertiary Students* Human Learning, 4, 127 – 142

White, R. J. (1999) *Head Transplants* Scientific American Presents, 10, (3), 24-26

http://www.isoc.org/internet-history/
http://www.commerce.net/
http://www.freeserve.com/
http://www.lineone.net/
http://www.ukerna.ac.uk/
http://www.lycos.co.uk/
http://www.yahoo.com/
http://www.bubl.ac.uk/
http://www.askj.com/
http://www.niss.ac.uk/

http://www.qmark.com/
http://www.eql.co.uk/assessor.htm/
http://webtester.weber.edu/
http://www.microsoft.com/
http://www.ucaid.edu/
http://www.cuteftp.com/
http://www.focus.ac.uk/
http://www.caacentre.ac.uk/
http://www.ntu.ac.uk/vc/vcinfo.html/
http://www.ucisa.ac.uk/
http://www.becta.org.uk/
http://www.eu.microsoft.com/uk/
http://www.equilibrium.com/
http://www.matchware.net/
http://www.webct.com/
http://www.wbtsystems.com/
http://www.hud.ac.uk/comentor/
http://www.cti.ac.uk/
http://www.tltp.ac.uk/tltsn/cases.html/
http://www.tltp.ac.uk/tltp/
http://www.ncteam.ac.uk/fdtl/
http://www.danware.com/
http://www.mailbase.ac.uk/
http://www.jtap.ac.uk/
http://designserver.mae.cornell.edu/cuseeme.html/
http://www.mindtrail.com/
http://www.le.ac.uk/castle/